ROGER FENTON
PHOTOGRAPHER OF THE CRIMEAN WAR

By the same authors:

THE HISTORY OF PHOTOGRAPHY
THOSE IMPOSSIBLE ENGLISH (with Quentin Bell)

By Helmut Gernsheim:

LEWIS CARROLL — PHOTOGRAPHER
JULIA MARGARET CAMERON
MASTERPIECES OF VICTORIAN PHOTOGRAPHY
THE MAN BEHIND THE CAMERA
NEW PHOTO VISION
TWELFTH CENTURY WALL PAINTINGS AT HARDHAM
    AND CLAYTON (with Clive Bell)
FOCUS ON ARCHITECTURE AND SCULPTURE
BEAUTIFUL LONDON

ROGER FENTON

PHOTOGRAPHER OF THE
CRIMEAN WAR

His Photographs and his Letters from The Crimea

With an Essay on his Life and Work by

HELMUT AND ALISON GERNSHEIM

London
SECKER & WARBURG
1954

Made and printed in Great Britain
by
William Clowes and Sons Limited
London and Beccles
and
first published 1954
by
Martin Secker & Warburg Limited
7 John Street, London
W.C.1

All half-tone blocks used in this book were
made by the Northern Photo Engraving Co. Ltd.

FOREWORD

THIS documentation of the Siege of Sebastopol in word and picture is largely Roger Fenton's own, preceded by an account of his life and a critical appreciation of his photographic work.

Some years ago we acquired for our collection of nineteenth-century photographs Roger Fenton's own set of Crimean War pictures—360 in all and, as far as we know, the only complete set in existence. From them we have selected sixty-six of the most interesting scenes of camp life, portraits of generals and officers, and views of Balaclava and the heights before Sebastopol which were the seat of the allied armies during and after the siege of the town. Fenton was obliged to return to England before the end of the siege, so, in order to complete the pictorial documentation of the war, we have included six photographs by James Robertson, taken after the withdrawal of the Russians on 8th September 1855, which vividly record the destruction of the Russian forts.

Accompanying Fenton's and Robertson's photographs, of which only a few have so far been published, are Fenton's hitherto unpublished letters from the Crimea to his family and to William Agnew of Manchester, who financed the undertaking for the sole right of publishing the views, in a similar way to that in which P. & D. Colnaghi, the London print-sellers, financed the work of the artist William Simpson.

The twenty-one letters which Fenton wrote to his wife, to his elder brother, and to his publisher, between arriving at Gibraltar on 27th February 1855, and 25th June off Constantinople on the way back, were copied by the family into a letter-book, now also in our possession. They required slight cutting for publication, for Fenton usually sent Agnew shorter descriptions of the more important events about which he wrote in detail to his wife, and in order not to mar the continuity of the story these duplicated passages have been omitted. When pressed for time, Fenton wrote only one letter, with the request for copies to be passed on. He ends a letter to Agnew: "Will you be so kind as to send a copy of this to my father, and ask him to send it on to my wife? I have asked them to send you copies of anything interesting, as by writing only one letter, I have time to send a much fuller account than if I wrote several to all who expect to hear from me."

The letters were written in instalments during several days, and the date at the beginning of them is not necessarily that on which they were begun, or even finished. It is astonishing that Fenton still had enough energy to write detailed accounts at the end of a strenuous day, or in snatches between his work and other engagements. That under such conditions he occasionally got mixed up in the date or the day of the week, left out a word or misspelt names of places and people is only human. Or perhaps the copyist, wearying of the length of the letters, now and then slipped up. These small points have been corrected, and we have also introduced paragraphs and punctuation non-existent in the letter-book. With these exceptions, which we did not consider important enough to require indication in the text, the letters are printed as Fenton wrote them. Explanations added by us are printed in italics.

In the same way in which we have included a few photographs by James Robertson, to complete the Crimean story we felt that the letter from Fenton's brother-in-law, Captain Edmund Maynard, who took part in the final assault on the Redan, was of sufficient interest to round off Fenton's account, as it does in the letter-book, which formerly belonged to Joseph Fenton, Roger Fenton's elder brother.

31st March 1954 HELMUT AND ALISON GERNSHEIM

LIST OF ILLUSTRATIONS

Part I

ROGER FENTON'S LIFE AND WORK

It is a hundred years since the invasion of the Crimea by the allied armies, English, French and Turkish, 57,000 men in all—the largest expeditionary force that had ever set out for war overseas. With it, the Russo-Turkish war, which for many months had been waged in the Danube basin, entered a new phase. The purpose of the expedition was to take the important naval base of Sebastopol, constructed by an English engineer, Colonel Upton, and his sons, in eleven years of incessant labour.

After the battle of the Alma on 20th September 1854, in which the Russians were routed, the British Commander, Field-Marshal Lord Raglan, wanted to attack Sebastopol from the north side, but the French Commander, Marshal St. Arnaud, did not consider it expedient to assault the town without first getting down the enemy's fire by the use of siege guns. The allies by-passed Sebastopol, the English occupied Balaclava and the French Kamiesh Bay as supply ports, and the armies took up positions on the plateau between Sebastopol and Balaclava. The bombardment of Sebastopol which took place on 17th October was, however, not followed by a successful assault, and the allied armies settled down to a long siege, for which they were ill-prepared.

Like Cassandra's, the gloomy prophecies of Lieut.-General Sir George Cathcart, Commander of the 4th Division, were ignored. Exactly a fortnight before he met his death on the field of Inkerman he wrote to his wife:

> Camp of 4th Division.
> Heights above Sebastopol.
> 22nd October 1854.

> This siege is a long and tedious business. The Russians are making a most gallant defence and we have given them time to prepare for us. Had we attacked them as I wished when I first came on here with my Division, that is, as soon as the whole army might have come up, they had not then recovered the defeat of the Alma and were not prepared for us. It was then an open town, but we have given them time to build up the most formidable entrenched positions possible,

which I saw growing up for three weeks under my nose *without a shot being fired to disturb them*, and now we are surprised to find that our supposed superiority in artillery and engineering is all a mistake. The ships made an attempt the other day, but can do nothing and got hardly used. God knows how it will end, and His will be done, but I believe we must go and take the bull by the horns and put an end to this business, but that would have been a much easier job a month ago than now. The weather is very fine, but about the 15th November they say intense cold commences and we could not live here.*

How correct General Cathcart was soon became apparent. A terrible hurricane swept Balaclava on 14th–15th November, destroying twenty-one transport and supply vessels in the harbour, inflicting great loss of life, and of vital food supplies, fodder for horses, tents and winter clothing for the British army. The subsequent suffering of the troops through exposure, malnutrition and insanitary conditions is too well known to need stressing here. The siege was, indeed, much longer and more tedious than General Cathcart could ever have imagined in October 1854— the allies were sitting in front of Sebastopol for eleven months, and did not succeed in taking the town until September of the following year.

If the Crimean War is memorable for the charge of the Light Brigade, Florence Nightingale and Russell of *The Times*, it is equally notorious as the most futile war ever fought, and the most fantastically mismanaged. In many respects, it was the last of the old wars, with dandy officers, purchasable commissions and mortar balls; in others, it is the first of the modern wars, with telegraphic communication, supply railway, efficient nursing and field kitchens, and the first to be covered by photographers and newspaper reporters.

But whilst the services of Florence Nightingale, Alexis Soyer and Sir William Howard Russell have formed the subject of a number of books, the work of Roger Fenton, photographer of the Crimean War, has hitherto been ignored by historians. Yet Fenton's are the first war photographs that have come down to us, and his name, like Russell's, will for ever be linked with this extraordinary episode in our history, for it was their reporting and recording of it in word and picture that made both famous almost overnight. Yet if we consult the Dictionary of National Biography, we search in vain for some information about Roger Fenton, though the activities of William Simpson, the war artist, and Alexis Soyer, the cook, are enumerated in detail. The D.N.B. lists, however, another Roger Fenton, a Doctor of Divinity (1565–1616), the first ancestor of the subject of this book of whom we have any knowledge. To Roger Fenton, D.D., was entrusted the translation of the

* This extract was sent by Lady Georgina Cathcart to a friend and is now in the authors' possession.

Epistles for the Authorized Version of the Bible published in the reign of James I. He was the author of several theological works, preacher at Gray's Inn, and rector of St. Stephen's, Walbrook, in the City of London, where he is buried.

Dr. Fenton had in his possession Lower Crimble, Lancashire, which was sold by his son, but bought back by a great-grandson and thereafter remained family property, eventually passing to Joseph Fenton (1765–1840), grandfather of Roger Fenton.

Joseph Fenton had two sons, John and James, by his wife Ann Kay of Limefield House, near Bury, Lancashire. On the death of his father, James (1740–1819), Joseph founded a bank in Rochdale in partnership with Eccles, Cunliffe and Robey. Later on he took his sons into partnership, and the bank became known as Fenton & Sons. In 1826 Joseph Fenton entered on another business venture—a cotton mill which he built on the bank of the river Roch. Hooley Bridge Mills, near Rochdale, was an important manufacturing enterprise. The building alone was said to have cost £1,000 for every yard of the fabric, and it was 300 ft. long, 200 ft. wide and five storeys high! Roger's grandfather was a progressive man and insisted that the works should be fireproof (hence the high building cost) and illuminated by gas— then still a novelty, the gas being made on the premises. The firm, whose business was the spinning and weaving of fustian and cotton, was called Fenton & Schofield, the latter being managing partner.

Joseph Fenton also invested his money in property, adding in 1820 to the family estate Crimble Hall, another estate in Lancashire, Bamford, with Bamford Hall, and in 1829 the Manors of Ribchester, Dutton and Bayley, which he bought from Cardinal Weld.

By enterprise and mercantile skill Joseph Fenton amassed a fortune, and when he died in 1840 left his two sons property worth half a million or more. John Fenton, Roger's father, inherited Crimble Hall, and James (1793–1857), his uncle, Bamford Hall; both also received an equal interest in the family bank and the cotton mill.

John Fenton (3rd July 1791–25th July 1863) had three sons and a daughter by his first wife Elizabeth Apedaile of Newcastle: Joseph (1817–1873), Roger (1819–1869), William (1820–1905) and Elizabeth. Soon after the death of his wife in 1830, John Fenton married the beautiful Hannah Owston of Brigg in Lincolnshire, by whom he had thirteen more children.

On the incorporation of the Borough of Rochdale in 1832, Roger's father was elected M.P. and sat as a Liberal in the first Reform Parliament. In the election of 1835 his previous Conservative opponent was successful, but on the latter's death two years later John Fenton was again returned to Parliament in the by-election, retaining his seat in the general election of the same year, and continuing to represent Rochdale until his retirement from Parliamentary life in 1841. John Fenton was also a Justice of the Peace for the County of Lancashire and the West Riding of Yorkshire.

As neither Roger's father nor his uncle James took an active interest in the family businesses in later years, the interest in the cotton mill was divided between Roger's elder brother Joseph and his cousin Joseph, whilst Roger's younger brother William and the same cousin Joseph took over the bank. Both firms were then supposed to be fabulously wealthy, but the family fortunes began to decline when Roger's brother, who had the management of the mill, wanted to have his own way in substituting steam-power for water-power, and, it is said, tried to get the whole concern into his hands. This family dispute naturally caused great embitterment. Separate valuations were made, and eventually arbitrators were appointed, but no agreement could be reached, and a lawsuit between the cousins resulted. It was the beginning of the end, for until judgment could be obtained, business at the mill ceased, the machinery depreciated, the three hundred workers' houses gradually became tenantless, and in time mill and houses presented the dreariest spectacle of ruin and decay, where once there was wealth, comfort and pride. All this happened over a period of nearly twenty years, after which the machinery had to be sold to defray expenses, and finally the whole business was swallowed up by the insatiable monster of the law. "Thus a really splendid fortune", runs a contemporary report, "or several splendid fortunes, have been thrown away by sheer stupidity, or something worse." From that time, the star of the Fenton family, which had seemed to be in the ascendant for half a century or more, began to grow dim. In 1878 the bank failed, and on the death of Roger Fenton's step-mother in the same year, Crimble Hall was sold in order to be able to pay creditors 20s. in the pound. Thus within a few years the downfall of the family fortunes was complete.

As already mentioned, Roger Fenton was born at Crimble Hall, Lancashire, in March 1819, the second child of John Fenton, M.P., by his first wife Elizabeth Apedaile.

At the beginning of 1838 Roger and his brother William began their studies at University College, London. After taking a Master of Arts degree, Roger became a pupil of Charles Lucy, an historical painter whose picture "The Meeting of Milton and Galileo" had attracted much attention in 1840.

About 1841 or '42 Fenton went to Paris to continue his studies as a pupil of the then celebrated painter Paul Delaroche, in whose studio, by the way, another well-known painter-photographer, Gustave Le Gray, received his art training. It was Delaroche who on first seeing a daguerreotype in 1839 had declared hysterically, "From today, painting is dead!" He soon took a more sober view when he discovered the "immense service" rendered by photography to art, and in his official report to Arago on the value of Daguerre's invention stated, "The painter will obtain by this process a quick method of making collections of studies, which he could not otherwise procure without much time and labour and in a style very far inferior, whatever his talents in other respects." Following his master's teachings, Fenton adopted photography with eagerness, probably obtaining his first instruction from Delaroche himself. During his training Fenton seems to have realized that he was not good enough an artist to make painting his career, and so about 1844 he returned to London to study the law, and was called to the Bar. He did not practise as a barrister, however, but became a solicitor, with an office at 50 King William Street, City. About 1847 Roger Fenton married Grace Maynard, by whom he had three daughters, Eva, Rose, and Annie Grace. The two latter became painters and exhibited at the Royal Academy.

In spite of his new career, Fenton did not give up painting and photography. For three consecutive years he had a canvas accepted by the Royal Academy: judging from the titles, they were typical Victorian anecdotal subjects which we would nowadays designate as trash. In 1849 he exhibited an illustration to Tennyson's "May Queen": "You must wake and call me early." The following year the title was: "The letter to Mamma: what shall we write?"; and in 1851: "There's music in his very steps as he comes up the stairs."

Since his return to England Fenton had become acquainted with the calotype, the photographic process on paper invented by Henry Fox Talbot. Talbot's method had the great advantage over Daguerre's that one could print any number of positive copies from a negative, as we do today. The soft sepia to purplish-brown prints gave broad effects similar to mezzotints. For this reason, as well as the greater simplicity of the process, artists and amateurs preferred photographs on paper to the sharp, minutely detailed and mirror-like surface of daguerreotypes.

When in the autumn of 1847 a number of amateur calotypists formed the Photographic Club in London, Fenton became one of the dozen members. The other eleven of this group, who used to meet once or twice a month at each others' houses to compare results and exchange ideas and prints, were Peter Wickens Fry, the founder; Robert Hunt, F.R.S., Keeper at the Museum of Practical Geology and a leading authority on photography in its early days; Frederick Scott Archer, sculptor, and inventor of the collodion process; Dr. Hugh W. Diamond, Superintendent at the Surrey County Lunatic Asylum; Sir William J. Newton, R.A., miniature painter; Peter Le Neve Foster, barrister, and secretary of the Society of

Arts; Joseph Cundall, publisher; Frederick W. Berger; Hugh Owen; Charles Vignoles, F.R.S., civil engineer; and Edward Kater, F.R.S.

At that period no organization of a more extensive character could be envisaged because the number of photographers was small. Both Daguerre's and Talbot's processes were patented in England, and until 1852 this fact very much retarded the progress of photography in England as compared with France. Ill feeling about patent restrictions increased when it transpired that photographers in England could not avail themselves of the albumen-on-glass or the waxed paper processes, recently invented and freely published in France by Niepce de Saint-Victor and Gustave Le Gray respectively, unless they took out a licence from Fox Talbot, the inventor and patentee of the calotype, who claimed every new photographic process, however different from his own, to come under his patent.

In 1851 there occurred, however, two events which were soon radically to change the position. The first was the Great Exhibition, which included the first important display of photographs. As a result, lovers and students of the art in all parts of England were brought into contact with the work of Continental and American photographers. For many, it was an eye-opener to the isolation in which they had been working, for they saw specimens of processes about which they had so far only read but had been unable to employ. As in other fields, the International Exhibition greatly stimulated the dissemination of new ideas, and the development of novel methods, and since the pleasure of giving and receiving instruction was mutual, the desire arose before long to "unite all those gentlemen whose tastes have led them to the cultivation of this branch of modern science" in a full-scale photographic society.

Frederick Scott Archer's publication of the collodion or wet-plate process in March 1851 was the second and still more important event in popularizing photography, for it constituted not only an improvement on all previous methods, but was the first process free from patent restrictions—at least, nobody at the time imagined that Talbot could possibly see in it a likeness to his calotype.

Feeling that the time was ripe for the establishment of a photographic society, Roger Fenton went to Paris in October 1851 to study the organization of the Société Héliographique—the first photographic society in the world—which had been founded the preceding January. He communicated a detailed report on its activities to *The Chemist* in February 1852, and the following month published in the same journal his "Proposal for the formation of a Photographical Society", which was circulated to all photographers whose addresses were known. Fenton envisaged a society on the lines of other learned societies, with a regular meeting place, a journal, a reference library and exhibitions, and he also suggested an annual album to which each member should contribute a photograph, rightly believing that such a collection would form an invaluable record of the advance of photography for future generations.

However, his efforts were thwarted because no agreement could be reached with Fox Talbot on the question of patent rights. Talbot, whom Roger Fenton, Robert Hunt and other members of the Calotype Club (as the Photographic Club was sometimes called) tried to persuade to abandon his monopolistic attitude, was quite prepared to play his part by giving a free licence to every member of the society to practise the art for his own amusement, but he at the same time imposed a number of conditions which the committee found unacceptable, and so the hopes for an independent society were, for the time being at least, dashed to the ground.

Realizing that "the existence of the patent was the great obstacle, not only to the formation of the society, but to the improvement of the art itself", the committee, of which Fenton was the ruling spirit, unavailingly approached several well-known scientists, including Michael Faraday, Charles Babbage and Sir John Herschel, with the request to persuade Fox Talbot to relinquish his patent rights. The Society of Arts, of which Fenton was a member, solicited their members' signatures to an appeal to Talbot, in the belief that the negotiations might be helped "by a letter signed numerously and influentially". The committee finally asked Sir Charles Eastlake and Lord Rosse, the Presidents of the Royal Academy and of the Royal Society respectively, to use their influence, and after a joint appeal from them, Talbot on 30th July 1852 relaxed his patent rights, still reserving to himself, however, the licensing of professional portraiture.

Nothing now stood in the way of the formation of a photographic society except Fenton's absence in Russia, whither he had gone to take some photographs for Charles Vignoles of the work in progress on the suspension bridge over the Dnieper at Kiev, which Vignoles had under construction for Czar Nicholas I. After completing his task, Fenton decided to make use of the opportunity to take some views of Kiev, St. Petersburg and Moscow, the domes of the Cathedral of the Resurrection in the Kremlin being the gem of the whole set (Pl. 2). Like all the other pictures, it was taken by Gustave Le Gray's waxed-paper process, in which Fenton was said to have been one of the most successful operators in England.

During Fenton's absence, Joseph Cundall proposed to the Society of Arts to hold a photographic exhibition before Christmas, and this suggestion was agreed to by the council on 17th November. It was the first public exhibition in Britain solely devoted to photography, and its success was said to be mainly due to the exertions of Fenton, who was back in time to assist in the arrangements, and read a paper at the opening soirée on 22nd December, "On the present position and future prospects of the art of photography."

The soirée was a great social event (Pl. 12) and a great event for photography. During the five weeks of preparation the surprisingly large number of eight hundred photographs had been brought together, affording a good idea of the condition of the new art at the time, for all the then known processes, with the exception of the daguerreotype (which was only employed by professional portraitists) were represented.

In the closing paragraphs of his paper Fenton reverted to his idea for the establishment of a society, which he said "is within one step of complete organisation, and awaits only the general co-operation of the whole body of photographers to enter upon an active and useful existence".

Encouraged by the widespread interest which the exhibition aroused (it was kept open until 29th January 1853 instead of only one week as planned), Fenton called a public meeting at the Society of Arts on 20th January 1853 to inaugurate the Photographic Society. At this meeting Sir Charles Eastlake, P.R.A., was elected President of the new Society, Fox Talbot having previously declined an invitation to fill this office. Sir Charles Wheatstone, Sir William Newton and Earl Somers became Vice-Presidents and Roger Fenton accepted the post of Honorary Secretary. All the members of the Photographic Club became founder-members. Thus the Photographic Society was born, the *doyen* of the thousands of photographic societies which exist today all over the world; for though preceded in foundation by the short-lived Société Héliographique, the Royal Photographic Society of Great Britain can look back on an unbroken record which makes it the oldest existing photographic society in the world.

On 3rd March 1853 appeared the first issue of the Journal of the Photographic Society under the editorship of Arthur Henfrey, F.R.S., and on 3rd January 1854 Eastlake and Fenton had the honour of conducting the Queen and Prince Albert round the first exhibition organized by the Photographic Society, at the Society of British Artists in Suffolk Street. Nearly 1,500 photographs were on view—the Victorians believed in arranging everything on an imposing scale! In 1855 followed the first annual album, and thus within two years all the main points of Fenton's programme for *the promotion of the art and science of photography*, the express object of the Society's foundation, were realized. It is scarcely credible that no tribute should have been paid to Roger Fenton during the centenary celebrations of the Royal Photographic Society, the officials of which like to claim that its foundation is due to Prince Albert, although the authors have more than once pointed out that the Society itself awarded Fenton a medal "as founder" in 1866.

It was no doubt due to the friendly relations between the Prince Consort and Roger Fenton that he and the Queen consented to become patrons of the Photographic Society in May 1853, four months after its foundation, though the official request naturally came from the President, Sir Charles Eastlake. Fenton was commanded to Buckingham Palace on several occasions between 1853 and Prince Albert's death, to photograph the Royal family, and it is very likely that it was he who initiated the Royal couple into the intricacies of the "black art" (as it was called on account of the black stains caused by nitrate of silver), for the Queen and Prince Albert took up photography with great enthusiasm, and had a dark-room constructed at Windsor.

Some of the photographs which Fenton took of the Royal family in 1853 are rather intimate family pictures: groups of Prince Albert with the children, and the children in *tableaux vivants* (Pl. 7). The latter the Queen regarded as unsuitable for publication (or perhaps the grown-up Princes and Princesses felt that these pictures were not compatible with Royal dignity) for when, long after Fenton's death, a relation unwittingly published one, she objected and asked for the negatives to be destroyed; yet somehow a few of these amusing photographs escaped destruction. As the Royal children grew older, it was, of course, easier for Fenton to arrange artistic groups (Pl. 8 & 9), and the many photographs which he took of the Royal family and the Royal residences, Buckingham Palace, Windsor Castle and Balmoral, testify to the frequency of his visits.

Fenton remained honorary secretary of the Society until February 1856, when at his own request a paid official was employed to take over the ever-increasing duties of secretary, now to be combined with editorship of the Journal as a full-time job. "I find that the child is becoming too troublesome for the father to manage, that it needs a strong hand to keep it in order and to rear it. During the three years that I have been secretary to the Society, it has grown in a manner which has surpassed my utmost expectations. . . . We are now become one of the institutions of the country." With these words Fenton summed up an achievement that must largely stand to his own credit.

Fenton retained his seat on the Council until May 1856, when he was obliged to resign this position, with four other prominent photographers—William Lake Price, Philip H. Delamotte, T. F. Hardwich and Charles Vignoles—because they had become council members of a commercial body, the Photographic Association. Fenton remained a member of the Society until 1862, and was elected a Vice-President in February 1858. He served on several committees appointed by the Society to examine specific photographic problems, foremost among them the causes of the fading of photographs. On account of his legal and photographic knowledge he was also chosen to sit on the Society of Arts' committee set up in 1858 to consider amending the existing law of artistic copyright, and it was due to his insistence on the claim of photography to recognition in the Fine Arts Bill that, four years later, the copyright of photographs was secured by an Act of Parliament. The battle was not won without occasional heated engagements. "Photography a fine art!" exclaimed a well-known painter. "Why, it is entirely dependent on camera and chemicals." "In a like manner," rejoined Fenton, "as the painter is dependent on pencils, colours and canvas."

PHOTOGRAPHY OF THE RUSSO-TURKISH WAR

The principal event of Fenton's career was his expedition to the Crimea in 1855. He is usually called "the first war photographer", but this is a fallacy. This designation applies to Karl Baptist von Szathmari, an amateur painter and photographer living in Bucharest, of whom it was remarked that "he became a painter because he loved the arts, and a photographer because he was a painter".

On the outbreak of the war in Wallachia, von Szathmari wanted to photograph the types and uniforms of the Russian army of occupation. His well-known artistic talent was sufficient recommendation to the Russian generals for them to sit to him. He photographed the Commander of the army, Prince Gortchakoff, Generals Osten-Sacken, Budberg, Kotzebuë, Liprandi, Count Orloff and others, and obtained from them permission to take his camera to the camp.

When the Turks in their turn occupied Bucharest, von Szathmari photographed their Commander-in-Chief Omar Pasha and other generals, and camp scenes. He also followed the warfare in the Danube basin in his photographic carriage, and his adventures with it are not unlike some of the experiences Fenton was later on to have in the Crimea with his van. Early in April 1854, for instance, von Szathmari wanted to photograph the quarantine station at Oltenitza. He had just set up his apparatus when he was startled by an explosion, and a few seconds later, by another. It became clear that his wagon had drawn the fire of the Turkish garrison, but not wishing to abandon the view he was taking, the photographer bravely stood his ground. Hardly had he packed up his camera than a third cannon ball, better aimed than the previous ones, tore up the ground a few paces away, covering him with sand.

Von Szathmari showed an album of about two hundred photographs at the

Universal Exhibition in Paris, 1855, where they were much admired. They do not seem to have been published, nor were they ever exhibited in England, and for this reason they have hitherto escaped the notice of every historian of photography. As we have not seen any prints, nor even reproductions, of Szathmari's photographs, we cannot give any opinion on their quality, but in order to see Fenton's achievement in proper perspective it seems essential at least to mention every attempt to document the Russo-Turkish War in photographs—and there were several.

Here in England, the first suggestion to make use of photography "to obtain undeniably accurate representations of the realities of war and its contingent scenery, its struggles, its failures and its triumphs" was made in *The Practical Mechanics' Journal* in January 1854. Photographers, it was suggested, should be attached both to the naval and military expeditions (though England was not yet a belligerent), for "the dimly allusive information, which alone the conventional works of the painter can convey, is powerless in attempting to describe what occurs in such operations, whilst a photographic picture brings the thing itself before us. By its instrumentality the Commander-in-Chief can send home to his government dispatches of the most convincing accuracy."

Not many weeks passed before the suggestion was acted upon. When the "Hecla" sailed with the fleet to the Baltic on 11th March 1854, Captain Scott took with him Gilbert Elliott, an amateur photographer. Elliott took views from the ship of Wingo Sound and the fortress guarding it, and it is said that the fortress was so clearly depicted in the photographs that an engineer officer declared he could determine the bearing of every gun and correctly lay down a plan of attack.

When France and Britain entered the war at the end of March, the British Government decided to attach a small photographic staff to the army, and appointed Captain (later Major) John Hackett of the 77th (East Middlesex) Regiment to take charge of it. From papers at the Public Record Office it transpires that Captain Hackett (who was Deputy Assistant Quartermaster-General of the expeditionary forces) contracted on 29th May 1854 with a civilian photographer named Richard Nicklin, an employee of Dickinson & Co. in New Bond Street, London. The agreement was for six months, to be extended thereafter from month to month, the rate of pay being 6s. a day, plus rations and other allowances. In addition, Nicklin was very generously given a free passage to Turkey! Corporal John Pendered and Lance-Corporal John Hammond, both of the Royal Sappers and Miners, Woolwich, were selected to act as Nicklin's assistants, and were to receive their regimental pay of 2s. a day (with usual deduction for rations). After a few days' instruction in photography, they embarked on 11th June for Varna, taking with them sixteen cases of photographic equipment. These contained one large and one small camera, two lenses, a dark-tent, eight bottles of collodion, and numerous other chemicals, empty bottles and dishes, four printing frames, two plate-holders, two camera stand tops, six tripod stands and an unspecified quantity of glass plates and printing paper.

There exists no information about Nicklin's photographic work either at Varna or at Balaclava, which the British occupied on 26th September. It must be presumed lost with all three photographers, who were on board the transport "Rip van Winkle" when it foundered, together with twenty other transport and supply ships, in the harbour of Balaclava during the hurricane in November 1854. Captain Hackett thereupon applied for replacement of photographers and equipment, and two young officers, Ensigns Brandon and Dawson, were sent in the spring of 1855 to the Crimea, with new apparatus and supplies, having received a month's training from one of the leading London portrait photographers, J. E. Mayall. Their photographs were reported, in May 1869, to be preserved at the War Office "in a deplorable condition", and were apparently subsequently destroyed, for a search made at our request at the War Office, the Public Record Office, the United Service Museum and the Imperial War Museum revealed no trace of them.

Tolstoi, who was in the army at Sebastopol during eight months of the siege (November 1854–July 1855) is supposed to have taken some photographs there: they are at any rate said to be ascribed to him in the Tolstoi Museum in Moscow. In spite of repeated requests we have not, however, succeeded in obtaining from the Soviet Embassy in London nor from the British Embassy in Moscow any confirmation of this fact, nor any copies of the photographs.

ROGER FENTON'S EXPEDITION TO THE CRIMEA

William Howard Russell's revelations in *The Times* in the autumn and winter of 1854–5 of the appalling conditions suffered by the troops, due to gross mismanagement, roused the conscience of the nation, and undermined confidence in the Government's ability effectively to prosecute the war. In one of his outspoken dispatches from the camp before Sebastopol Russell wrote on 25th November:

It is now pouring rain—the skies are black as ink—the wind is howling over the staggering tents—the trenches are turned into dykes—in the tents the water is sometimes a foot deep. Our men have not either warm or waterproof clothing—they are out for twelve hours at a time in the trenches—they are plunged into the miseries of a winter campaign—and not a soul seems to care for their comfort, or even for their lives. These are hard truths, but the people of England must hear them. They must know that the wretched beggar who wanders about the streets of London in the rain, leads the life of a prince compared with the British soldiers who are fighting out here for their country.

(1st December) The dead, laid out as they died, are lying side by side with the living, and the latter present a spectacle beyond all imagination. The commonest accessories of a hospital are wanting; there is not the least attention paid to decency or cleanliness—the stench is appalling—the foetid air can barely struggle out to taint the atmosphere, save through the chinks in the walls and roofs, and for all I can observe, these men die without the least effort being made to save them.

Though the Government tried to counter these allegations, denials and explanations were of no avail: the official casualty lists bore out Russell's reports. Seven-eighths of those who died succumbed to cholera or to the hardships of the winter, whilst only one-eighth died of wounds. The storm broke, and on 1st February 1855 Lord Aberdeen's Government announced its resignation.

Whether Roger Fenton's expedition to the Crimea in the same month had any political significance or was merely a commercial enterprise, or a bit of each, is difficult to judge. It is certain that the expedition was made under the patronage of Queen Victoria and Prince Albert, and with the assistance of the Duke of Newcastle, Secretary of State for War. On the other hand, it was financed by the Manchester publisher Thomas Agnew & Sons, who wanted pictures of the people and scenes of historical interest, with the object of selling them to the public. It is clear that, in order not to offend Victorian ideas of good taste, Fenton had to avoid portraying the ravages of war, and it is in this light that we have to view his entire *opus* of 360 photographs. They are in striking contrast to Russell's reports, which, it must be remembered, concern the very worst period of the war, when the suffering of the troops was at its greatest following the loss of winter clothing and supplies in the November hurricane.

Meanwhile, Florence Nightingale and her nurses, and other parties, had arrived in the East to look after the sick and wounded, new supplies of winter clothing and tents had arrived, and a commission was trying to improve the extremely insanitary conditions. Meanwhile also spring had come early, and the notorious quagmire had dried up, making it possible again to transport supplies from the harbour to the camps. A further improvement had been brought about by constructing a supply railway from the harbour as far as Kadikoi, and soon right up to Headquarters camp. So by the time Fenton arrived at Balaclava on 8th March 1855 conditions were decidedly better, though it is evident from his letters that he did not lack opportunities to record the dismal side and even the horrors of war, had he wished. But would the public in England have bought any horrifying pictures of prostrate bodies lying in the field? Decidedly no. What they wanted to see was: "A cantinière tending a wounded man" (Pl. 54), "The Sanitary Commission" (Pl. 41), "The cookhouse of the 8th Hussars" (Pl. 34), "A quiet day at the mortar battery" (Pl. 52), a convivial party of French and English officers entitled "L'entente cordiale" (Pl. 31), men in sheepskin coats (Pl. 35 & 71), views of the encampments and cheerful regimental groups (Pl. 45 & 79). Photographs like these were more powerful proof than words that most of the remedies Russell had called for had been put into effect, and they re-assured the public that at last the men were properly cared for after their terrible sufferings the preceding winter.

Fenton embarked on 20th February 1855 from the East India Docks, London, on the "Hecla", having been provided with a passage by the Duke of Newcastle, the Minister for War, and Sir Morton Peto, M.P. He took with him a photographic van and two assistants: William the handyman and cook, and Marcus Sparling, a former corporal in the 4th Light Dragoons, as driver and to look after the horses. Both were, of course, to help with the photographic work, cleaning the glass plates, printing, mixing chemicals and possibly coating the wet collodion plates, but only Fenton actually took the pictures. From his letters it transpires that both assistants were rather unreliable and too fond of the bottle. Indeed, within five years Sparling was dead. Inflammation of the liver was the doctor's verdict. It was a pity, for Sparling was a gifted man. He was the inventor of an ingenious portable magazine camera (c. 1850) and author of a comprehensive textbook on photography (1856). Fenton had originally intended to leave him at home to manage the business in his absence, but William seemed so helpless, "having been lamenting with his friends in the Irish way with whisky, that I did not feel quite safe to rely upon him alone, and took both".

Both assistants and the photographic van had already been employed by Fenton the previous autumn on a photographic tour of Yorkshire, which resulted in the publication of a portfolio of eighteen views. Originally a wine-merchant's vehicle in Canterbury, Fenton had it converted into a caravan fitted up for living, cooking, sleeping and dark-room work. "When it entered into the service of Art, a fresh top was made for it, so as to convert it into a dark room, panes of yellow glass, with shutters, were fixed in the sides; a bed was constructed for it, which folded up into a very small space under the bench at the upper end; round the top were cisterns for distilled and for ordinary water, and a shelf for books. On the sides were places for fixing the gutta-percha baths, glass-dippers, knives, forks and spoons. The kettle and cups hung from the roof. On the floor, under the trough for receiving waste water, was a frame with holes, in which were fitted the heavier bottles. This frame had at night to be lifted up and placed on the working bench with the cameras, to make room for the bed, the furniture of which was, during the day, contained in the box under the driving-seat.''

From the experience obtained on the tour in Yorkshire, several modifications were made in the construction of the carriage, until it finally assumed the form in which it appears in the photograph taken in the Crimea on the day it travelled down the ravine called ''The Valley of the Shadow of Death''. ''The picture'', relates Fenton, ''was due to the precaution of the driver on that day, who suggested that as there was a possibility of a stop being put in the said valley to the further travels of both the vehicle and its driver, it would be showing a proper consideration for both to take a likeness of them before starting'' (Pl. 14).

On several occasions Fenton's van came under fire. In the bare country it stood out for miles on account of its size and light colour (so as not to absorb heat) and formed a target for the Russians, who doubtless thought it was an ammunition wagon. But Fenton remained cool in the presence of danger, resourceful and persistent in pursuing the aims he had set himself.

At a meeting of the Photographic Society Fenton enumerated the vast amount of other photographic equipment he had taken with him: five cameras of different sizes and several lenses, of which the largest had a focal length of 20 in. and diameter of 4 in., a stock of about 700 glass plates contained in grooved wooden boxes, several chests of chemicals, a still for distilling water, three or four printing frames, gutta-percha baths and dishes. In addition to the photographic baggage, he took a sleeping tent, several boxes of preserved meat, wine and biscuits, harness for three horses to be bought in Gibraltar, one of Price's candle stoves, carpenter's tools and a great many other things likely to be useful. The whole lot filled no fewer than thirty-six cases ''which took up so much space on Blackwall Pier as to make me think with rueful forebodings of the sort of resting-place they were likely to find on the shore at Balaclava'' (Pl. 16).

Arriving at Balaclava on 8th March, Fenton at once experienced that extra-ordinary lack of co-ordination which was a feature of the whole campaign. Merely to get the van and equipment disembarked meant spending days running from pillar to post, from the Admiral to the captain of the port, and from him to the captains of the ships in the harbour. ''From everyone I received kind attention and promises of assistance, but I always found that either the promised barge was loading with shell and would not be empty for two days, or that unluckily somebody else had just taken it without orders, or that the barge was there but the men that belonged to it had just been ordered elsewhere. It was then that I saw that if I could get none but official assistance, Sebastopol would be taken probably vi et armis, but not by photography.''

When he finally disembarked—by private enterprise—the difficulties began all over again with the allocation of a hut to store the equipment, the acquisition of a saddle, and the requisitioning of fodder for the three horses he had bought in Gibraltar, the number of which so astonished the Commissary-General that he asked: "Are you a general's office?"

Next, the horses turned out to be riding-horses not broken in for draught, and Fenton had to ask the railway authorities and the artillery to lend him some whenever he wanted to move his van. Little wonder that the exasperated photographer at last gave vent to his feelings in a letter to Agnew: "I don't think, if I could have foreseen all the difficulties of my task before setting out, that I should have had the courage to come, but by pitching into them one by one, I suppose they will be mastered."

It was a week before Fenton was able to take his first picture, and for a fortnight he photographed in the neighbourhood of Balaclava, taking views, and portraits in his hut, with an improvised background of curtains. Indeed, much at Balaclava had to be improvised. There was no ink, and it had to be manufactured out of soot and vinegar. There were no washerwomen, and some officers sent their linen as far as Malta to be laundered!

"The whole place is one great pigsty" is Fenton's summing-up. "At present eighty sheep are slaughtered every day in the vessels in harbour alone, and the entrails thrown into the water alongside. All over the camp, animals wanted for food are killed close to the tents, and the parts not used are rotting for days." How anyone could expect to keep the army in a healthy condition when this sort of thing was going on, is beyond imagination.

In order to avoid the necessity of explaining the purpose of the carriage, the words "Photographic Van" were painted on it in large letters, with the result that crowds of all ranks flocked around. "Everybody is bothering me for their portrait to send home", Fenton complains. "Were I to listen to them and take the portrait of all comers, I should be busy from now to Christmas, and might make a regular gold-digging in the Crimea, but I am very anxious to get up to the front."

At the end of March he took the van out of the town to the Guards and Cavalry camps near Kadikoi, where for several days he took portraits, groups and views. The van was then dragged by stages up to Headquarters, sometimes by six artillery horses, at others by men who hoped to get their picture taken as a reward. Up to this time Fenton had lived on board the "Hecla" in Balaclava harbour, but up on the plateau he relied for food and shelter on the hospitality of friends, sometimes sleeping in a general's marquee and sometimes on the bare ground. He was of a friendly nature and got on well with everybody, and this, of course, made his path smooth. For several weeks he lived at General Sir John Campbell's, who treated him just as if he were one of his staff. Breakfasting and dining in turn with the various English and French top brass hats at whose quarters he was photographing at the time, Fenton saw and heard much which he would never have known had he been placed in any official position. General Bosquet was particularly friendly and discussed with him the whole conduct of the war. "I could not help now and then thinking what a queer *tableau vivant* I was forming part of, *tête à tête* with one of the most celebrated men of the day, discussing the conduct and capacity of the great guns of our acquaintance, with much more freedom than if I had formed part of a special mission."

Compared with Russell or Simpson, or indeed with any other reporter or artist attached to newspapers, Fenton enjoyed unusual privileges resulting from his letters of introduction from Prince Albert to Lord Raglan and other commanders in the field. Whereas Russell complained that Lord Raglan never spoke to him and that he was only regarded as a kind of camp follower, Fenton took precedence over Prince Edward of Saxe-Weimar at Lord Raglan's dinner table. There he met Lady George Paget. "She is very pretty and is at present the *belle* of the Crimea. Lord George Paget was there too, and for once got very chatty; champagne had something to do with it. I was on Lord Raglan's right and Lady G. Paget on his left, so I had plenty of conversation with her."

Fenton was rather fond of eating and often describes to his wife with gusto the menu of the swell dinners with champagne and cigars at the generals' and officers'— dinners which we would nowadays only expect at a luxury hotel, and which stand in great contrast to the miserable grub the ordinary soldier had to put up with, and until Alexis Soyer had his field kitchens in working order (June 1855) even had to cook himself.

His impressions of the generals are quite revealing: "Sir Richard England may be a bad soldier, but he is not a bad rider." "General Pélissier is a very good personification of the French army, for he is rough in his manners, though not without a certain *bonhomie*. He cares nothing for the sacrifice of life and does not seem troubled with scruples of any kind. His face has an expression of brutal boldness something like that of a wild boar." "General Bosquet said it was not possible for anyone to have a greater dislike of war than a soldier like him, whose life for the past twenty years had been spent in burying his friends." Of Lord Cardigan he wrote to his publisher: "If you have not got a portrait of him, I should recommend you to take no trouble about it, as you will before long have a very different account of his conduct from that he has himself given. I have heard men and officers in the cavalry regiments discussing his conduct, and not one has a good word to say for him."

There was no censorship and anyone could write what he liked, though Fenton cautions his publisher that it would be damaging to him were any of his letters published in the newspapers. Yet he is comparatively mild in his criticisms of the prevailing muddle, always remembering that he is in the Crimea with special privileges.

In spite of his friendly relations with General Bosquet, Fenton could not resist having an occasional dig at the French. "They make much fuss, and seem to attack every night, but one generally finds each morning that the Russians have made some slight advance towards them, instead of being gradually driven into the town (Sebastopol)."

His letters give vivid glimpses of camp life—and what a conglomeration of nationalities had taken the field against Russia, or were working for those who did: British, French, Turkish, Egyptian, Algerian, Sardinian, Corsican, Maltese, Piedmontese, Montenegrins, Croats, Tartars, German and Swiss mercenaries. It was a hotch-potch of nations not unlike the United Nations in Korea.

While Fenton was up at Headquarters, Napoleon III and Empress Eugenie paid a state visit to London. The personal meeting of the monarchs was intended to cement the alliance and further the prosecution of the war, and indeed two Councils of War were held during the five-days' visit, during which Queen Victoria was quite captivated by the charm of the Imperial pair, whom she had previously regarded as upstarts. "The impression is very favourable", wrote the Queen to her uncle the King of the Belgians. "There is great fascination in the quiet, frank manner of the Emperor, and *she* is very pleasing, very graceful, and very unaffected." The alliance was progressing more swiftly than anyone could have foreseen. "I know of *no* one who puts me more at my ease, or to whom I felt more inclined to talk unreservedly, or in whom involuntarily I should be more inclined to confide, than the Emperor! . . . wonderful it is that this man—whom certainly we were *not* over well-disposed to—should by force of circumstances be drawn into such close connection with us, and become *personally* our friend, and this entirely by his own personal qualities."

Queen Victoria invested the Emperor with the Order of the Garter, they attended a military review, a ball at Windsor Castle, a lunch at the Guildhall, heard "Fidelio", and on the last day of the visit, 20th April, the party went to the Crystal Palace, lately rebuilt at Sydenham, where they were enthusiastically received by a huge crowd. The occasion was recorded by two photographers—Henry Negretti of Negretti & Zambra, and T. R. Williams, who had put their cameras on a stage erected in the gallery opposite the Royal dais. In spite of the comparatively long exposure necessary, they succeeded in taking the picture by choosing a quiet moment in the proceedings—the speech of welcome (*Pl. 15*).

During the spring the light and temperature in the Crimea were everything that a photographer could desire, but as spring began to change into summer, the difficulty of getting successful pictures became in every way greater. The actinic power of the light was less and Fenton complained that he had taken pictures in England in the spring more rapidly than at any time in the Crimea. With the same collodion and with the nitrate of silver bath in apparently the same condition as in the spring, the time of exposure became gradually longer, and as it got hotter still, it became very difficult to keep the nitrate bath in good working order. It was difficult, too, in the great heat to clean the glass plates properly, because impurities upon the glass, which at a lower temperature would have done no harm, became centres of chemical action, causing spots or streaks in the negative. It was necessary now to thin down the collodion to a much greater extent than was necessary in England, and even with this precaution, when working with the larger plates, 12 in. × 16 in. and 16 in. × 20 in., the wet collodion would sometimes dry where first poured on, before the liquid had time to spread evenly over the rest of the plate. Also the coating often became nearly dry in the short time needed to carry the slide containing it to the camera and back again, and then the developer would not, when poured on the plate, run at once all over it. The collodion was only sensitive while in a moist state, which restricted the photographer's range from his dark-room, whether a van or a portable tent. In the dry heat of the Crimea, Fenton could probably not have carried the plate further than about a hundred yards from the van, for it had to be developed, as well as exposed, while still moist, and the plate would probably have been dry within five minutes.

To the technical difficulty of coating the plates was added the sheer physical discomfort of working in the intense heat in the stuffy van, aggravated by dust and a plague of flies. In spite of its light colour, the van grew so hot towards noon as to burn the hand when touched, and there were no trees to give shade. "As soon as the van door was closed to commence the preparation of the plate, perspiration started from every pore, and the sense of relief was great when it was possible to open the door to breathe even the hot air outside." Some idea of the heat may be gained from the fact that, when one day in the beginning of June the van door was left open, the sun shining into it blistered a gutta-percha funnel "as if it had been laid on the hot bars of a fireplace." Fenton laconically comments: "One drinks like a fish. I reckoned yesterday that I took seventeen tumblers of liquid, nine of which were tea, two champagne and the rest beer."

Soon he had to leave off working at ten o'clock in the morning, for quite apart from the fatigue, it was impossible to take any satisfactory portraits after that hour "for the glare was so great from the sky and burnt-up ground, no one could keep his eyes more than half open." The famous Council of War of the three allied

Commanders-in-Chief in consultation on the morning of the taking of the Mamelon (7th June 1855) was photographed about 5 a.m. (*Pl. 76*).

Fenton now found that the distant hills, which during the spring were always distinct, and shone in the greatest variety of rich colour, gradually merged in the hot weather into one indistinct mass, melting into the hazy sky, and he was glad he had finished taking distant views in April and could now concentrate on portraits and groups. The haze is noticeable in a number of pictures, and it gives some of them quite a warlike air, as if the smoke of battle were hanging in the background.

Actually, battle scenes were quite ruled out at this period of photography, and Fenton was not able to fulfil the wishes of the young lady who, according to *Punch*, wrote to her fiancé in the Crimea: "I send you, dear Alfred, a complete photographic apparatus which will amuse you doubtlessly in your moments of leisure, and if you could send me home, dear, a good view of a nice battle, I should feel extremely obliged. *P.S.* If you could take the view, dear, just in the moment of victory, I should like it all the better." Battle scenes were in fact first photographed during the 1914–18 war, though gelatine dry plates, which were twenty times faster than collodion, had made instantaneous action pictures (but not of fighting) possible during the Boer War.

All groups had to be carefully arranged in order to avoid movement. When this was impossible, as for example in the railway yard or at the cavalry encampment, we sometimes see the blurred outline of a few men or horses. Exposures varied between three and twenty seconds in fine weather, depending on the size of the plate, the focal length of the lens, and its aperture. It is a proof of Fenton's skill that, in spite of the comparatively long exposures, the great majority of his photographs successfully convey the impression of being snapshots. There is never a row of people obviously waiting to be photographed and staring at the camera, but casual groups in which some slight action takes place, such as reading an order (*Pl. 80*), passing a bottle (*Pl. 31*), officers at lunch (*Pl. 38*) or making their dog beg (*Pl. 45*), or General Bosquet pointing out the line of attack to his staff, (*Pl. 58*) one of whom seems to be taking notes.

Portraits of officers and men form a high proportion of the photographs, but whilst Fenton naturally wished to perpetuate the distinguished officers of the allied armies who took part in the memorable siege of Sebastopol, and took great delight in photographing the foreign troops and labourers in their picturesque uniforms and costumes, he found it a bore to be constantly bothered to take portraits of officers and men in whom he was not interested, "yet if I refuse to take them, I get no facilities for conveying my van from one locality to another". (Fenton himself enjoyed dressing up in a Zouave uniform he borrowed from General Bosquet's

Division, had himself photographed in it by Sparling, and for a lark published it with the title "Zouave, 2nd Division" (*Pl. 1*). He also obtained a kepi from the same source, in which he was photographed after his return to London.)

Work progressed slowly, and Fenton sought to defer the resumption of his photographic work for the British Museum authorities, with whom he was under contract. "There is far more work here than I could do in six months. I am sorry that I am obliged to return so soon." Agnew was getting anxious that public interest might be on the wane by the time he could publish the pictures, and urged Fenton to send the negatives to him, but that was far too risky, and in order to keep him quiet, and the English public interested in the things which were to come, Fenton sent him from time to time batches of prints, which were shown to the Queen and Prince Albert, and copied in the form of woodcuts in the *Illustrated London News*.

Fenton did not have a high opinion of the sketches made by Edward Goodall, the artist of this newspaper. He asked Agnew: "Have you seen that picture in the 'Illustrated London News' of Sebastopol from the sea? It has caused a good deal of astonishment and amusement here, as it is a regular 'Punch' sketch. Goodall's sketches seem to astonish everyone from their total want of likeness to the reality, and it is not surprising that it should be so, since you will see from the [photographic] prints sent herewith, that the scenes we have here are not bits of artistic effect which can be effectually rendered by a rough sketch, but wide stretches of open country covered with an infinity of detail."

Being himself a trained artist, Fenton had also taken his sketch-book to the Crimea, and in several letters refers to sketching, particularly on the expedition to Kertch at the end of May, when he left photographic equipment and assistants behind to see to the printing of the photographs so far taken. These water-colour sketches were executed for Lord Raglan, to whom he gave an eye-witness account, having returned by the first ship back to Balaclava, while the fleet pushed on to the Sea of Azov. It is amusing that Fenton joined this military expedition because he was feeling run down and wanted a change! But then many strange things happened in this curious war: the presence of officers' wives (*Pl. 42*) at the front, the race meetings, "T.G.s" or travelling gentlemen—private individuals who went to the Crimea in search of thrills and were free to wander about at the front and got passes to enter the trenches and batteries in a casual way.

Fenton was himself one of the onlookers when the French stormed the Mamelon fort on 7th June 1855, and when he heard that the great attack on Sebastopol was to take place, which everyone was confident would succeed, he stayed on and made preparations to photograph the town and the Russian forts that had withstood the siege for so long. With a number of officers and men he anxiously watched from

Cathcart's Hill the progress of the French assault on the Malakoff and the English assault on the Redan. After some hours it was evident that both attacks had failed. Deep gloom descended on the camps, for the casualties were heavy. "In our confidence of success", notes Fenton, "we had chosen this day in order that on the anniversary of Waterloo a victory common to both nations might efface from the minds of one the recollection of their former defeat, but we reckoned too proudly, and now the 18th of June will be a glorious day to the Russians. What's to be done now, no-one can guess, except that it will be a long time before the town is taken."

There was no talk of a fresh assault, and as he felt quite unequal to further exertion, Fenton took the first opportunity of a passage home. He had been in a poor state of health for some time, and depression at the loss of many friends in action on 7th and 18th June had aggravated his condition. Being afraid that the embarkation of the van might prove as troublesome as its disembarkation three and a half months earlier, Fenton sold it for £35, and the horses and other items which he did not wish to bring back to England were also disposed of.

On 26th June he sailed from Balaclava a sick man. Having lived for the previous month at Headquarters, which was in a very unhealthy condition, he was infected with the fresh outbreak of cholera to which Lord Raglan, General Estcourt and so many others fell victim at that time. Sparling and William took great care of him, and by good fortune he was spared and was well on the way to recovery by the time he arrived in England.

He was immediately commanded to Osborne for an audience with the Queen and Prince Consort, and owing to his weak state enjoyed the unusual privilege of lying on a couch in the Royal presence while recounting his adventures. In August, the Queen and Prince Albert paid a return state visit to Paris, and nothing demonstrates more clearly the importance of Fenton's work and the great interest his Crimean photographs aroused than the fact that they took with them about twenty of the photographs, which the Royal and Imperial couples studied together. Soon after, Fenton and William Agnew were asked by Napoleon III to present themselves at the Palace of St. Cloud, where they were received in audience on 12th September. They showed the Emperor the entire collection of 360 photographs. The Empress was unwell, expecting the Prince Imperial at the time and was in an adjoining room; it is reported, however, that whenever Napoleon saw a photograph which particularly pleased and interested him, he took it in to show her. During the audience, which lasted an hour and a half, the Emperor smoked cigarettes incessantly. Fenton and Agnew were asked to come again the next day, "for the Emperor was not able to satiate his curiosity in one long séance", as *The Times* Paris correspondent cabled on

13th September, adding: "His Majesty expressed to these gentlemen his satisfaction, and commanded them to prepare immediately a number of copies of the views."

During October 312 of Fenton's photographs were exhibited at the gallery of the Water Colour Society in Pall Mall and immediately afterwards were shown at several provincial centres. Everywhere the portraits and camp scenes aroused widespread public interest, and Dr. Thoms, editor of *Notes & Queries*, voiced the general opinion when he wrote on 6th October: "An exhibition of deeper interest

EXHIBITION

OF THE

Photographic Pictures taken in The Crimea,

By ROGER FENTON, Esq.

DURING THE SPRING AND SUMMER OF THE PRESENT YEAR,

AT THE

GALLERY OF THE WATER COLOUR SOCIETY,

Nᵒ 5, PALL MALL EAST.

OPEN FROM TEN TILL DUSK.

ADMITTANCE, ONE SHILLING.——CATALOGUES, SIXPENCE.

PRINTED FOR
MESSRS. THOMAS AGNEW AND SONS,
PUBLISHERS AND PRINTSELLERS TO HER MAJESTY, EXCHANGE STREET, MANCHESTER,
BY THOMAS BRETTELL, RUPERT STREET, HAYMARKET.

1855.

was never opened to the public. It is a pictorial and running commentary on the graphic narrative of 'The Times' special correspondent. The stern reality stands revealed to the spectator. Camp life with all its hardships, mixed occasionally with some rough-and-ready enjoyments, is realized as if one stood face to face with it; and after viewing with deep emotion the silent gloom which overshadows the 'Valley of the Shadow of Death', the eye rests with yet deeper feelings on the tombs on Cathcart's Hill."

"This series of photographs constitutes much the most interesting and valuable memorial of the Siege that could be given", said the *Art Journal*. "No verbal description can place before us with such palpable reality the persons who have figured in this memorable Siege, or the localities which constitute the widespread theatre of operations."

The photographs were published by subscription in parts between 1st November 1855 and 5th April 1856, Agnew subtly pushing the sales by insinuating (without foundation) that "more than 200 good impressions [from each negative] cannot safely be guaranteed". It is a matter of speculation how many were actually printed. Fenton's pictures are comparatively rarely met with, which would indicate that the edition was limited, but it would not be safe to go beyond that statement and hazard a guess. Subsequently the photographs were issued in a number of red cloth portfolios, each containing a dedication page "To her most gracious Majesty Queen Victoria, this series of incidents of Camp Life [or Historical Portrait Gallery, *or* Views of the Camps, *or* The Photographic Panorama of the Plateau of Sebastopol, *or* The Photographic Panorama of the Plains of Balaclava and the Valley of Inkerman], photographed during the spring and summer of 1855 by Roger Fenton, Esqre, is most respectfully dedicated by her Majesty's most grateful subjects and servants Thomas Agnew & Sons." On the outside the portfolios bear the following inscription in gilt letters: "Photographs taken under the patronage of her Majesty the Queen in the Crimea by Roger Fenton, Esq. Agnew & Sons, publishers, Manchester."

Altogether 360 views, groups, portraits, panoramas, etc., were published, but as Fenton had taken two or three different views of some subjects it was stated that a good general selection of portraits and views comprised 160 photographs, which cost 60 guineas. The Panorama of the Plateau of Sebastopol consists of eleven numbered photographs and an explanatory outline woodcut. The Panorama of the Plain of Balaclava and the Valley of Inkerman comprises eight numbered photographs with explanatory outline woodcut. The size of the photographs, which could also be bought singly at prices varying from 10s. 6d. to one guinea, varies from half-plate to 15 in. × 12 in.; they are all on large white mounts (26 in. × 20½ in.) bearing, in addition to the title, name of the photographer, date of publication and publisher's name and address, the following names of retailers: P. & D. Colnaghi, London; Moulin, Paris; Williams & Co., New York.

In his "Narrative of a photographic trip to the seat of war in the Crimea" which Fenton gave to the Photographic Society on 3rd January 1856, he mentioned that he had hoped to add to his collection of views "photographs of the scenes since so ably depicted by Mr. Robertson". James Robertson was superintendent and chief engraver of the Imperial Mint at Constantinople, and an enthusiastic amateur photographer, well known for his views of Constantinople, Athens, Malta and other places in the Mediterranean, published in London in the 'fifties.

Robertson arrived in the Crimea shortly before the fall of Sebastopol. He went over much of the ground already covered by Fenton, such as the view of Balaclava from the Guards' camp (Pl. 29), but the chief value of his sixty or so pictures lies in the fact that the majority of them form a continuation of Fenton's, and show the result of the siege. We see the indescribable confusion in the Redan, scene of the great struggle on 8th September (Pl. 84), the bomb-proof shelter of the Russian generals in the Redan (Pl. 82), the telegraph station erected by the French on the remains of the Malakoff tower (Pl. 81), the French trenches between the Mamelon and the Malakoff (Pl. 56), the mantelets (a coil of rope forming a high collar round the naval gun) protecting the Russian gunners in the Barrack Battery (Pl. 83), and many similar scenes.

Robertson's views of Sebastopol, showing the ruined city, and the docks, and Forts Nicholas, Constantine, Paul and Michael, and the bridge of boats across which the Russians withdrew on the night of 8th September, are less interesting. Ruined buildings do not evoke in us the excitement of novelty which they had for the Victorians.

There is every indication that Robertson's expedition was a private enterprise, for most of his photographs (which were taken by the albumen-on-glass process, and are usually very faded) were issued unmounted and consequently bear no publisher's stamp or printed inscription, though they usually have his signature scratched on the plate. Some sets, however, were issued by Agnew's and bear their imprint. His collection was shown in February 1856 at the studio of the well-known daguerreotypist W. E. Kilburn in Regent Street, London.

Still another English amateur paid a visit to the Crimea in the autumn of 1855. Like Robertson, George Shaw Lefevre (later Baron Eversley) took some views of Sebastopol immediately after the withdrawal of the Russians. Twelve of them were published at his own expense in April 1856, and sold by the London printseller J. Hogarth. Shaw Lefevre's work, however, falls far below the standard set by Fenton's and Robertson's, and we doubt whether the Nightingale Fund was greatly swelled by the profits arising from the sale of the prints.

Irked by the fact that the French had shown less enterprise than the English (*The Manchester Guardian* stated after Fenton's and Agnew's visit that "The Emperor seemed surprised that that which could only have been undertaken by the Imperial Government in France, should be the speculation of a private firm in England"), the French Government somewhat belatedly sent some photographers to

Sebastopol—or possibly they only despatched apparatus to officers known to be amateur photographers. We have seen in French collections a few photographs of groups and camp scenes taken after the end of the siege and bearing the imprint of Colonel Charles Langlois, L. Méhédin & Martens, and Durand-Brager & Lassimonne. Colonel

No. 1355.

CATALOGUE
OF THE
ENTIRE REMAINING COPIES
OF
SIMPSON'S SEAT OF WAR IN THE EAST,
(COLNAGHI'S AUTHENTIC SERIES)
AND
ROGER FENTON'S PHOTOGRAPHIC PICTURES
OF THE
WAR IN THE CRIMEA,
TOGETHER WITH THE ORIGINAL GLASS NEGATIVES;
ALSO
A MAGNIFICENT ASSEMBLAGE
OF
CHOICE MISCELLANEOUS ENGRAVINGS,
PICTURE GALLERIES & BOOKS OF PRINTS,
ALL SPLENDIDLY BOUND.

Which will be Sold by Auction, by

SOUTHGATE AND BARRETT,
AT THEIR ROOMS, 22, FLEET STREET, LONDON,
On MONDAY EVENING, DECEMBER 15th, 1856,
and SEVEN FOLLOWING EVENINGS,
(SUNDAY EXCEPTED,)
AT SIX FOR HALF-PAST SIX O'CLOCK PRECISELY,

———

May be Viewed and Catalogues (price 1s. each, returnable to purchasers) had at the Rooms.

Jean Charles Langlois, owner of a well-known panorama in Paris, was the first to apply photography to the making of panoramas. At the end of 1855 he went to the Crimea, where he stayed four months. From the top of the Malakoff he took photographs of the positions occupied by the armies, and after his return to Paris he used these as a basis for his panorama "The Taking of Sebastopol", first exhibited in 1860.

After the fall of Sebastopol war faded gradually into peace, but it was not until 30th March 1856 that the peace treaty was signed in Paris. The Parisian portrait photographers Mayer & Pierson commemorated the event with a photograph of the fifteen plenipotentiaries taking part in the congress, England, France, Turkey, Russia, Austria, Prussia and Sardinia being represented. As a mark of their satisfaction with this highly interesting historical photograph (*Pl. 85*), the Emperors of France and Austria each presented Mayer & Pierson with a gold snuff-box ornamented with diamonds and the Imperial initials! (Who doubts that the mid-nineteenth century was literally the golden period of photography?)

With the conclusion of peace, public interest in the war waned rapidly, and it is by no means certain that Agnew's venture, which cost him several thousand pounds, really yielded the golden harvest which the *Art Journal* prophesied. The same is probably true of Robertson's photographs, and certainly of Simpson's sketches. Fenton's and Robertson's negatives, as well as small stocks of unsold prints of their photographs, were sold by auction by Southgate & Barrett, London, on 20th and 23rd December 1856, whilst 22nd December was solely devoted to the sale of the large remainder of complete volumes of Simpson's "Seat of War in the East"—no fewer than 1,919 copies.

In the spring of 1856 Roger Fenton resumed his work for the Trustees of the British Museum, photographing classical sculpture (*Pl. 4*), Old Master drawings, skeletons and general views of some of the galleries. He was the first photographer admitted to the British Museum, and calotype and albumen prints from his collodion negatives were subsequently on sale to the public at the South Kensington Museum. Mounted copies were also published at intervals between 1856 and 1858 by P. & D. Colnaghi & Co.

In the 'fifties photographers were much troubled by the fading of photographic prints, and the great desideratum was to discover a process by means of which photographs could be reproduced in permanent printing ink, suitable for book illustration, instead of having to glue actual photographs in between or on the text pages. Hitherto the chief fault of all photomechanical printing processes was the lack of half-tone which renders photographs so pleasing, but in 1854 Paul Pretsch, manager of the Imperial Printing Establishment in Vienna, evolved an electro-photo-engraving process which promised to overcome the difficulty. Pretsch came to England to exploit his invention, which he called "Photogalvanography", and early in 1856 formed a company, but another ten months passed by before the first plates were published. When at last there appeared in November the first number of

"Photographic Art Treasures, or Nature and Art illustrated by Art and Nature", everyone who saw it was "perfectly crazy with astonishment and delight", for this first publication of photographs in printing ink marked the dawn of a new era in the history of photography and printing—photo-engraving.

The advantage of photo-engraving over hand-engraving as regards accuracy hardly needs stressing, but the advantages of cheapness and speed may be less obvious. Whereas the Photogalvanographic Company required six weeks to make a printing plate (subsequent photo-engraving processes were greatly speeded up), the work of hand-engraving paintings took several years. W. P. Frith's "Railway Station" occupied the engravers four years, and Raphael Morghen needed six to engrave Raphael's "Transfiguration". Consequently the cost of good engraved copper plates ranged from several hundred to several thousand pounds, according to the fame of the engraver and the time taken over the work. A Paris print-seller paid as much as 3,000 guineas to have Paul Delaroche's "Execution of Lady Jane Grey" engraved, and prints from hand-engraved plates had to be priced at several guineas, whereas prints from photo-engraved plates could be sold for a shilling or so.

Altogether six parts of "Photographic Art Treasures" appeared at irregular intervals until September 1857, in the unusually large format 15½ in. × 23 in. Each part contained four plates of popular subjects by well-known photographers such as Fenton, Lake Price and Rejlander, and reproductions of paintings. The prints were issued in three qualities: choice proofs, proofs and prints, the prices for the parts varying between 10s. 6d. and 5s.

A month or two before the publication of the first number Fenton was appointed manager of the photographic department and chief photographer to the company, which published a large number of miscellaneous subjects by him, including a series of views of Bolton Abbey.

Unfortunately, photogalvanography was not yet in a sufficiently perfect state to render it independent of costly retouching at the hands of the engraver, and the firm went out of business in 1859.

Like most photographers of his time, Fenton took up stereoscopic photography when the craze for 3-D. pictures set in in the mid-'fifties. In January 1858 the London publisher Lovell Reeve brought out the first book illustrated with stereo photographs, "Teneriffe: an Astronomer's Experiment" by C. Piazzi Smyth, the Astronomer Royal for Scotland. It was followed the same year by "Stereoscopic Views in North Wales", a series of twenty-one photographs by Roger Fenton and accompanying text by him. On 1st July 1858 appeared the first number of "The Stereoscopic Magazine: a gallery of landscape, scenery, architecture, antiquities and natural history", which continued monthly for five years. It was the first and only periodical ever published with stereoscopic photographs, each number having three illustrations, and many were by Fenton. Yet another book illustrated by him was "The Conway in the Stereoscope" (1860), with twenty photographs, and text by J. B. Davidson. Fenton also took many photographs for William and Mary Howitt's "Ruined Abbeys and Castles of Great Britain and Ireland", the photographically-illustrated edition of which was published by A. W. Bennett, London, in two volumes, appearing in 1862 and 1864.

For his many photographic tours Fenton had another travelling dark-room constructed soon after returning from the Crimea. A great many of the views which he took for the stereoscope were also photographed with one of his larger cameras, usually 16 in. × 12 in. or 20 in. × 16 in. These large pictures earned him the distinction of being the greatest master in landscape photography in Great Britain. In 1855 Paul Périer, writing of Fenton's prints at the Universal Exhibition in Paris, had called him "an outstanding example of the perfect union of artist and technician", and in 1856 Thomas Sutton, the hypercritical editor of *Photographic Notes*, wrote after looking over a "glorious" collection of new prints: "In this superb series of views, principally of the romantic scenery of Scotland and Yorkshire, will be found many in which Mr. Fenton has surpassed the best of his former work. There are marvellous natural skies and distances, effects of rain and haze, foliage and water, rugged rocks, mountain passes, glens, waterfalls and ruins deliciously rendered . . . Further than this the art of photography cannot possibly be carried, until either the means of producing the natural colours, or processes absolutely instantaneous are discovered . . . It is worth a journey from any part of Great Britain to the Metropolis, to see so superb a collection of artistic photographs, and to learn how much photography can really accomplish."

Fenton did not confine himself to depicting the scenery of England, Scotland and Wales. He always ventured into new fields. His extensive series of exteriors and interiors of English cathedrals shows that he was as much a master of architectural as of landscape photography.

What a fine picture is his view of the terrace and park of Harewood House! (*Pl. 3*) When exhibited in 1861 it was criticized as one of the worst pictures Fenton had ever taken. Yet the "offensive series of parallel lines one above the other, without much apparent recession", to which the reviewer objected, is the very feature that, by its boldness of conception, appeals most to us today.

Influenced by the taste of the period, Fenton was also occasionally tempted to portray anecdotal subjects by photography, as he had ten years earlier by painting. In contrast to contemporary critics who bestowed unstinting praise on these compositions, we regard his fancy pictures of people in eastern costumes as failures, because the English models at once betray by their stiffness and artificiality of pose that these costumes were utterly alien to them. This is just one more instance of the almost complete reversal of taste of present-day critics of photography and art alike, compared with the opinions expressed by their opposite numbers in the nineteenth century. Much of what they praised we condemn, and usually what they condemned we regard as the best inheritance from that rather perplexing age, at any rate in artistic matters!

But if Fenton's "Nubian Water Carrier" and "Egyptian Dancing Girl", and similar subjects which he showed at the Photographic Society's exhibition in 1859, have to be condemned as Victorian trash, he was so brilliant in all other fields that an occasional error of taste is soon forgiven.

At the exhibitions of 1860, 1861 and 1862 Fenton was prominent in a new branch—still-life photographs of fruit and flowers and game, of which we reproduce two of the finest (Pl. 10 & 11). These have a delicacy and texture equal to the finest seventeenth century Dutch still-lifes, yet though they were deservedly honoured by a medal at the International Exhibition in London, 1862, some of Fenton's compositions are rather overcrowded and not always very happy in grouping.

To mid-Victorians a comparison with George Lance's paintings was obvious. Here was the same accurate representation of fruit, foliage, flowers, and all the varied accessories of glass, china and drapery, for which this now forgotten painter (a pupil of Benjamin Robert Haydon) was once famous. One critic went so far as to claim that Fenton's photographs were reproductions of Lance's paintings, whilst another insinuated that Lance had composed some of Fenton's fruit studies. Considering that the majority of Victorian painters spent their time copying photographs, we are more inclined to think that it was the other way round, if, indeed, there is any connection at all. Several of Fenton's photographs were copied by artists without acknowledgment. "The Council of War" by Augustus Egg, A.R.A., is an exact copy of Fenton's picture, whilst T. Jones Barker's painting of the allied generals and other officers before Sebastopol—a group of some eighty officers of the British and French armies—is based on Fenton's portraits. A third example which comes to mind is J. H. Lynch's lithograph of W. H. Russell, also copied from Fenton's photograph.

In October 1862, at the height of his fame, Fenton suddenly startled the photographic world by the announcement that he intended to retire from photography and resume his former profession of the law. This news was received everywhere with unfeigned regret, and the Photographic Society, which owed its existence to Fenton's exertions, expressed the hope that it would still have the benefit of his advice for many years to come. Fenton never officially explained the reason for this surprising decision. According to Dr. Hugh W. Diamond, who followed him as secretary of the Photographic Society, Fenton gave up photography because he saw no future in it on account of the fading of prints. He told Diamond that one of his volumes of British Museum photographs had rapidly faded although another remained in good condition, and he could in no way account for the difference. The failure of the Photogalvanographic Company, which had given rise to great hopes, and the low status to which photography was relegated at the International Exhibition, 1862—it was classified under "Machinery"—were possible contributory causes. Like most photographers, Fenton was rather sensitive on this point, rightly regarding the decision as an insult to the young art. There may also have been still weightier grounds, for with the beginning of the rage for *carte-de-visite* portraits in 1860-1, thousands of cheap traders suddenly swelled the ranks of photographers to share in the most profitable craze that ever existed in photography. For a time the public entirely lost their taste for large portraits and views, which were naturally many times more expensive than the small mass-produced cards, bought by the dozen and priced in shillings. No serious artist could compete with such industrial methods, but *nolens volens*, photographers had either to conform to the new craze or find themselves driven from business. Unwilling to sacrifice quality and not being dependent on photography for his livelihood, Fenton may have chosen the second course rather than turn into a *carte* photographer, and he may have considered that a return to his legal practice in connection with the Stock Exchange demanded no compromise and was the best way out of the *impasse*.

Having made this decision, Fenton thought it wise to deprive himself of everything that might tempt him to revert to his past occupation, so in the middle of November his entire equipment, which included the second photographic carriage and thirty lenses, from the small stereoscopic to immense pieces of "photographic artillery" used for the production of negatives 3 ft. square, and nearly a thousand of his negatives, were disposed of at Stevens' Auction Rooms, King Street, Covent Garden.

Some of the large negatives were bought by Francis Frith, photographer and print-seller in Reigate, who soon after published several folio volumes of "The Works of Roger Fenton", each containing twenty of Fenton's best photographs (size 16 in. × 20 in.) in one particular field. Two of them, "Cathedrals" and "Landscapes", are in the collection of the Royal Photographic Society.

Fenton worked at his former office in the City until, after a short illness caused by hurrying to catch a train, he died on Sunday 8th August 1869 at the age of fifty. Unpunctuality is a trait for which, we are told, the whole Fenton family is noted, in contradiction to the motto on their crest, "Je suis prest". For over twenty

1. Roger Fenton in borrowed Zouave uniform

2. The Domes of the Cathedral of the Resurrection in the Kremlin

3. The Terrace and Park of Harewood House

5. Dr. E. Becker, with the Prince of Wales and Prince Alfred

4. Bust of Atys

7. The Royal children in a *tableau vivant*

6. The Royal family in 1853

8. The Princess Royal and Princess Alice

9. The Princesses Helena and Louise

10. Still-life of game

11. Still-life of fruit

12. Opening Soirée of Photographic Exhibition

13. "Hardships of Camp Life"

14. The Photographic Van
with Sparling on the box

15. Visit of Napoleon III

16. Head of Balaclava Harbour

17. Ordnance Wharf, Balaclava

18. Balaclava Harbour

19. The Genoese fort at the entrance to Balaclava Harbour

20. The Post Office, Balaclava

21. General view of Balaclava with hospital

22. The Railway yard, Balaclava

23. The Railway Yard, Balaclava

24. Lieut.-General Sir Henry John William Bentinck

25. Lieut.-General Sir George de Lacy Evans

26. Lieut.-General Sir Colin Campbell

27. Lieut.-General H.R.H. the Duke of Cambridge

28. The Cattle Wharf, Balaclava

29. View of Balaclava with Genoese fort

30. Encampment of the 71st Regiment

31. "L'Entente Cordiale"

32. Cavalry camp, looking towards Kodikoi

33. A dromedary

34. Cookhouse of 8th Hussars

35. Group of 47th Regiment in winter dress

36. Croats

37. Montenegrins

38. Major-General Garrett and officers of the 46th Regiment

39. Major-General James Bucknell Estcourt and staff

40. William Simpson, War Artist

41. The Sanitary
Commissioners

42. Captain Henry Duberly and "the dashing Mrs Duberly"

43. William Howard Russell
of *The Times*

44. "His Day's Work Over".   Lieut.-Colonel Hallewell and servant

45. Officers of the 71st Highlanders

46. Encampment of Horse Artillery

47. Officers and men of the 8th Hussars

48. The Tombs on Cathcarts Hill

49. The Remains of the Light Company 38th Regiment

50. Lieut.-General Sir John Campbell and Captain Hume

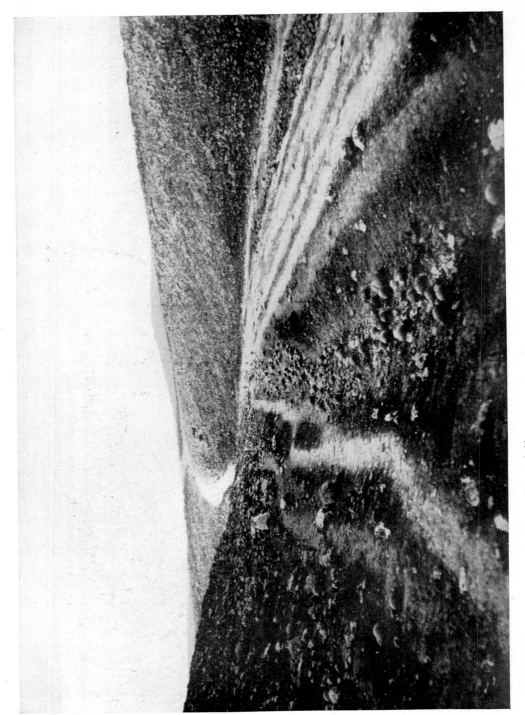

51. "The Valley of the Shadow of Death"

52. "A Quiet Day at the Mortar Battery"

54. Cantinière tending a wounded man

55. General Bosquet and Captain Dampière

56. The French trenches, with the Malakoff in the distance

57. General Bosquet's quarters, looking towards Mackenzie farm

58. General Bosquet and staff

59. Lieut.-General Sir Harry Jones

60. Lieut.-General Sir Henry William Barnard

61. The 57th Regiment

62. Allied camp on plateau before Sebastopol

63. Colonel Brownrigg and the captured Russian boys

64. Officers and gun-carriage

65. Field-Marshal Lord Raglan

66. Captain Hughes

67. Major-General James Bucknell Estcourt

68. Marshal Pélissier

69. Ismael Pasha receiving his chibuque

70. Lieut.-General Sir George Brown and staff

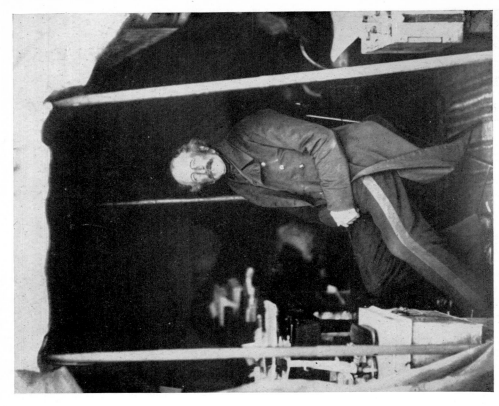

72. Lieut.-General Sir John Lysaght Pennefather

71. Captain Brown of the 4th Light Dragoons

74. The Provost-Marshal

73. A private in full marching order

75. Group at Headquarters (from left to right): Lord Burghersh, an A.D.C.,
Colonel Vico, Lord Raglan, Marshal Pélissier, a Spahi, an A.D.C.

76. The Council of War: Lord Raglan, Omar Pasha, Marshal Pélissier

77. Tartar labourers

78. English infantry
piling arms

79. At the camp of the 4th Dragoon Guards

80. Captain Walker read-
ing general orders

81. Remains of the Malakoff

82. Russian generals' bomb-proof shelter in the Redan

83. The Barracks Battery

84. Interior of the Redan

85. Plenipotentiaries at the signing of the Peace of Paris, 1856.
Seated (left to right): Baron von Hübner (Austria); Ali Pasha (Turkey); Earl of Clarendon (British
Foreign Secretary); Count Walewski (France); Count Orloff (Russia); Baron de Bourqueney
(France); Earl Cowley (British Ambassador)
Standing (left to right): Count Cavour (Sardinia); de Villamarina (Sardinia); Graf von Hatzfelt
Bey (Turkey); Baron Brunnow (Russia);

Part II

ROGER FENTON'S LETTERS
DURING HIS EXPEDITION TO THE CRIMEA

THE VOYAGE TO GIBRALTAR

Gibraltar,
February 27th 1855.

THE old Rock has got his cap on and looks very sleepy, not half so brisk as the last time I saw him; no doubt if he could speak he would say, "And you the same, old fellow."

We have had a weary passage. After leaving you we steamed down the river [Thames] till dark; when we were getting near the Goodwin Sands the pilot anchored for the night. It was a great pity, for the wind was blowing hard from the east and would have carried us down the Channel at a famous rate. Before dawn, however, we got out, and then began my troubles—it was the old story, seasick as if I had never been on salt water before. Towards dawn [21st February] I managed to get on deck, and though there was a good wind there was little sea. We kept alongside of England all night and then stood across the Channel towards the Bay of Biscay. The wind got fresh and the sea too, but still I kept up, though very sick, and managed to enjoy myself, for we were going at a fine pace with wind and steam.

Next day [22nd February] we were in the Bay of Biscay and I was floored. I managed to get on deck in the afternoon—in fact, the Captain dragged me up, as the sight was too fine to be lost. The ship was struggling along, jumping from wave to wave, frisking, groaning, rushing against the walls of water like a bull and being brought up shaking its head half stunned. The sea was white with foam as far as we could see. We got half across the Bay on that day, but in the night the wind changed and we found to our great dismay that the steam power of the engine was not sufficient, and we could do little more than hold our own. That day and the next I lay prostrate, groaning in spirit, unable to eat or drink. Sparling was if anything worse. William I heard was all right, which was very improper, considering the state his master was in.

When we got out of the Bay I got much better, though unable to eat or drink

35

except when lying down, and then only tea or biscuit. I am still very sick and unable to dress myself or do more than just crawl upon deck. We were never so near the land as during my last journey this way, never near enough to make out more than a faint outline, but there was plenty to do in watching water and sky. The gulls were wheeling about, and working hard in their vocation, now and then a porpoise rolled alongside out of the water and in again, and once a thrush came fluttering about the ship as if anxious for rest.

On the 26th we rounded Cape St. Vincent and then the wind, being turned a little to the north, became a good one for us and we were at the same time sheltered by the land. All the half-dead men in the ship rose up to different degrees of life. I actually sat up to dinner, in the cabin; had soup, roast fat pork, plum pudding and damson tart, and did not part with it. In the evening I intended to have written to you, but had convincing internal reasons for changing my mind and going to bed; thought of you all instead.

The Captain told me we should be at Gibraltar the next day [27th] but we were here so much earlier than I expected that I was not up to see the signal fired from the top of the Rock.

At Gibraltar. 27th February.

9 p.m. A regular jolly day. At 8½ a.m. I went on shore with the Captain to the fort, to the Governor's aide-de-camp. I found he had gone over the Spanish frontier to San Roque, a town six or seven miles off, where a lot of horses and mules were waiting for him to select for the Government. It was pouring with rain but I got a guide, and accompanied by Sparling set off on horseback after him. When we got to San Roque, with not a dry thread on us, we found Captain Lawson surrounded by horse dealers, mule drivers, etc. When he heard what I wanted he went round with me to the stables where there were the horses and mules rejected as undersized. I picked out a short-legged black horse 14½ hands, six years old, for which I paid £16. After looking at many others we got to the mules, but the Government had cleared out all worth having. Captain Lawson told me of some at Gibraltar which had been offered to him, so back we went.

My ride today after leaving the shore was up a hilly road bordered by hedges of aloes and great thickets of cactus. In coming back there was a beautiful view of the Rock, the top capped with mist, and beyond the bay covered with shipping there was a magnificent background formed by the mountains of the African coast. So much for the poetry of the situation. As far as the prose of it, they cannot get at my portmanteau, and if his Excellency the Governor should ask me to dine with him

I should be obliged to ask his Excellency to lend me a clean shirt. The steward has bought 1600 oranges for 16 shillings.

Fenton bought two more horses at Gibraltar, and set sail again the following day for Malta, where he sought out his wife's brother Edmund Maynard, a captain in the 88th Regiment. Maynard was an ancestor of the Countess of Warwick, who was one of Edward VII's friends.

FROM MALTA TO CONSTANTINOPLE

March 2nd 1855,
near Cape Matapan.

On arriving in Valetta harbour we were fought for by boatmen. Having learned that the 88th were quartered at the Auberge de Bonvière, I set off with eyes as wide open as the bright sun would allow, and chuckling inwardly at the prospect of a good day's sightseeing. The Auberge is beautifully situated close to the edge of the water in a little bay. Edmund had gone boating, so leaving word I would be back soon, I set off with my fellow voyagers to St. John's Church. Having seen many more magnificent churches and having heard so much of this from Edmund, I was somewhat disappointed at its first appearance, but found plenty of interest in the examination of the tombs of the Grand Masters. We walked all about Valetta. The brilliant sunshine, flowers in full bloom, and the novel architecture and varied costumes seemed like a frieze taken from the Arabian Nights. Having walked, admired and enjoyed to our hearts' content, we returned to the town and went to the post office, where I found the papers and your letter. Then we went to find Edmund. He accompanied us to the hotel, where we ordered dinner, and then went with us to the other part of the town. I left my name at the Governor's: they were all out, but Edmund was to dine there in the evening and would tell them I had come to offer to convey anything they might wish to send to Hallewell [Major Hallewell, 28th Regiment]. Before returning to dine we went on to the ramparts to see what was doing on board our ship, and while standing there, the "blue Peter", or flag saying the vessel was just going to sail, was put up. We were not going to be done out of a good civilised dinner, however, so made our way to the hotel, comforted the inner man in a deliberate manner, got quietly on board, and in ten minutes were steaming out to sea, the sun having just sank below the horizon as we lifted the anchor.

After the excitement and bustle of the day our quiet calm was really very refreshing. I read your letter with great delight, then went on deck to think about it, and got dreaming about the stars and the sea, whose breast was gently heaving

it seems like a new edition of the Tower of Babel. There appears to be considerable confusion in the Government arrangements, and they say that when the new commissioners come out it will make things still worse. I hear there is nothing new of any importance from the Crimea, except that the British troops are much more comfortable, and that some French general has been detected in correspondence with the enemy. [This seems to have been a mere rumour.]

To his wife he wrote two days later:

My last letter left off at my arrival at Constantinople by moonlight. I was up betimes in the morning to see the sun rise on mosque and minaret. After breakfast we called a caique, and the Captain and I went on shore to call at the English naval office. We came into a passage about a yard wide, and picking our steps along this in the midst of all sorts of abominations, we passed through an arch into another passage about two yards wide with booths and shops on each side, a gutter in the middle and horrible mountains of dirt every few yards. Sliding and stumbling along and wondering when we should get to a street, we got to a corner where another passage crossed ours at right-angles. Down this was pouring a stream of people, Turks, Jews, Armenians, frowsy women with veiled faces and bare legs, jaunty French soldiers, English sailors, and every minute a string of porters with their loads slung on poles came swaggering by, upsetting people and being upset themselves. Following the crowd, we came down to the waterside and found the men at the landing stage of the Custom House, the said stage being a wooden platform about the size of two dining tables. Here we learned that the last passage down which we had come was the main street of Galata. Calling at the naval office, we found Major Hackett, under whom the Photographic Corps were first placed when they went out. [See page 11.]

After lunch I went with Hackett to Stampa's, a man who keeps an universal shop for treacle, knives, Bibles and other groceries (!). He got us a Jew guide and we set off across the bridge to Stamboul, got horses on the other side and rode up to the bazaar, a place roofed in—all alleys and passages with shops on each side, the owner sitting cross-legged smoking on one corner of his bench. The Turks may be a grave people, but they made plenty of noise and fun in trying to sell their wares.

Dismounting to set to work seriously to bargain, Major or ''Banbashee'' Hackett, as he announced himself to them, wanted some red forage caps with gold embroidery, and he went from shop to shop in the search, accompanied by a crowd of fellows all eager to assist and share the plunder. When the caps were found, the owner asked two pounds each for them, whereat the "Banbashee" stormed and shook his knobbed stick in the man's face and the clatter of tongues became great, everybody assuring us that the Turk would be ruined if he took half the money, which the Major offered. At last an officious spectator shook the man by the shoulder, took the caps and handed them to us and in return took our money and placed it in the man's hand, and in conclusion made us a present of some perfumes lying on the stall—thus proving that in spite of our clever bargaining we had been done! I got a pair of velvet slippers and some attar of roses, the genuineness of which I have my doubts. There were several women shopping in the bazaar. The way they cover their faces, letting only their eyes be seen, is very coquettish, the more so as if their's is a good face the veil is of so transparent a material that the beauties it covers can be easily divined.

Leaving the bazaar, we rode to St. Sophia's Mosque and prepared to march boldly in, but we heard a cry of horror behind and some fellows came forward and made all sorts of signs and speeches for us to go back. Major Hackett told me, however, that the Sultan had given orders for the free admission of English and French, so we blustered in return (or rather Hackett did, who seemed to like the exercise) and they tried for what was, after all, their real object—"Backsheesh" —but in vain, and at last withdrew their opposition, only informing us that we must take off our shoes. This was no inconvenience as the whole floor of the church is covered with the richest Turkey carpets. I am not going to give you a description of the Mosque. I was much pleased with it, and though it is so vast and richly ornamented, it is at the same time remarkably light and airy. The traces of the Christian Church are yet very visible.

There was an old Turkish fellow sitting cross-legged on one side, surrounded by a circle of other men, all squatting, to whom he was expounding the Koran. As far as I could judge from what his tone and manner indicated, he seemed to be talking sensibly; there was no attempt at unction such as you see among the Roman Catholic ecclesiastics. The audience were very attentive and occasionally joined in some kind of response. Remembering that in their way they were worshipping God, I felt unwilling to keep my hat on, but they would have thought it disrespectful to have taken it off. Leaving this place we rode back to Pera and dined at Messerie's Hotel [L'Hôtel d'Angleterre, the best hotel] and slept there, as I was told it was unsafe to go down the narrow streets near the harbour after dark.

The next day [6th March] I called at the Embassy and delivered my letter from Prince Albert. Lord Stratford [Lord Stratford de Redcliffe Canning, the British Ambassador] was ill in bed but he sent me a very civil message, and I had an interview with Lady Stratford, whom I found very busy superintending the departure of

Miss Erskine [Superintendent of the Naval Hospital at Therapia] and of the Sisters of Mercy to Balaclava [Mary Stanley, sister of the Dean of Westminster, and her 46 Sisters and nurses who went first to Therapia and afterwards to the hospitals at Kullali and Balaclava].

Getting down into the port I found the ship ready for starting, and soon we were steaming up the Bosphorus; a beautiful sight it was, steaming by mosques, palaces, pretty villages and places famed in history. Rounding a projecting point where stood a very beautiful villa given lately by the Sultan to his son-in-law, there were some Turkish ladies at an open window who returned our salute with a right merry laugh. In Benos bay we saw the "Belle Poule", the Prince de Joinville's frigate—a very handsome vessel. At a quarter to four we were in the Black Sea and soon found the difference of temperature. Towards sunset a thick fog came on, the vessel seemed sailing through infinite space, nothing ahead, nothing all round. Next morning it was dull and wretched, my breakfast would not stop in its proper place, so I lay down all day and thought ruefully of things in general.

This morning [8th March] I was up by daylight, for land was in sight and speculation was afloat as to whether we should not float into Sebastopol by mistake. We are lying off the entrance to Balaclava with four other steamers and a brig, waiting until we are bidden to go in. Having satisfied my curiosity as far as the telescope will do it, I will proceed to satisfy yours. Purprinus, an officer, has just given us the news (how true, you will know better than I) that the Emperor of Russia is dead of an apoplectic fit [Nicholas I died 2nd March 1855], the said news having come by electric telegraph from Vienna. There is great speculation on board in consequence. Next we are told that there are 18 to 20,000 English troops effective instead of 10,000 as "The Times" said; that they have had beautiful weather for the last fortnight and are going on very well. With the telescope I can see on the hill to the right of the entrance a range of wooden huts looking like a hospital. It is washing day, and further back are a lot of tents mixed with huts, built and building. The hill looks trodden down, not a bit of green on it. Farther to the right the hills are covered with low trees which seem as if they could keep the whole army in fuel for months; I suppose they could not get at them for the Russians, though I can see no signs of the latter gentlemen. All along the beach where the barracks were, can be seen planks and broken masts stretching for more than a mile. [Relics of the hurricane which swept Balaclava on 14th–15th November 1854.]

The harbour of Balaclava was a fjord-like inlet of sea about ¾ mile long and less than 300 yards wide, hemmed in by rocky hills several hundred feet high. The entrance to the straits, invisible from the open sea, was commanded by an old

Genoese fort. The little town consisted of a few private houses and shops mostly on the east side of the harbour. The Greek inhabitants were forced to leave soon after the occupation by the English, because Lord Raglan learned of a conspiracy on their part to set fire to the British shipping and stores, but the Tartars were allowed to remain, and many of them worked on the loading of the supply railway, which by the end of March 1855 reached Headquarters camp. This railway, on which wagons were at first drawn by horses or mules, and by stationary steam engines at steep places, was eventually powered by ordinary railway locomotives. Some of the houses in Balaclava were destroyed by the troops in order to obtain fuel, others were taken down to make way for the railway terminus.

A mile and a half north of Balaclava was the village of Kadikoi, and on the nearby hill the Guards and Cavalry camp. From here, turning westward, the rough road climbed up to the bare 700-ft. high plateau, intersected by numerous ravines, on which the French and British armies were encamped. The British H.Q. was about seven miles from its supply base at Balaclava, the French supply base at Kamiesh Bay was more accessible. The nearest part of the British camp to Sebastopol was only about a mile and a half distant from the town, which was strongly defended on the south side facing the besiegers, the Russians having had time to strengthen their forts. The Redan (a work open at its rear) was one of the principal Russian works. The other, the Malakoff, or Round Tower, was continually strengthened with earthworks, though the upper part of the stone tower was ruined in the bombardments until at last nothing was visible above the level of the earthen defences. About 500 yards in front of the Malakoff was a green hill, the Mamelon Vert, on which on the night of 10th–11th March 1855 the Russians constructed another celebrated earthwork.

The siege of Sebastopol was incomplete: the north side of the town remained open owing to the presence of the Russian field army, 30–40,000 strong, and the Russians were able to bring reinforcements and supplies into the beleaguered city.

ARRIVAL AT BALACLAVA

After waiting outside the harbour for some three or four hours in obedience to a request not to go in without further orders, we got impatient, so did two or three other steamers, and all three quietly steamed in, and after a blowing up from the Port Captain we got squeezed into our places after some hours' work. No one, I think, ever saw so many vessels crowded together in so small a space as in this little harbour (Pl. 18); it is said there are 150 here now, and the Captain of the Port who succeeds in preserving any approach to order must be a man of ability.

Before the ship got to her berth I went on shore and landed on a real stone jetty without getting knee-deep in mud, and then stepped on to a rough stone road which will be in time a good macadamised one. On either side of this road, however, there is plenty of evidence of what a filthy swamp the streets must have been a few weeks back. The Post Office (Pl. 20) was just in front, the ground floor of which was a stable and the upper floor accessible by stone steps outside; this is the way in which the best houses are made. Having looked in vain for some of the people to whom I had letters of introduction, I strolled up the village to look about me, and faith, there was no want of things to make one stare. The emptying of Noah's Ark could not have been half so queer a sight. Had it not been for the long row of English graves at the head of the harbour one might have thought it a huge fair.

First of all the railway attracted one's notice. It is open as far as Kadikoi, a village a mile and a half off. Navvies and Turks were working together loading wagons and emptying ballast (Pl. 23), and evidently on good terms with each other. Leaving the road to the right, we followed a road which crosses a stream and gradually ascends to Kadikoi. We were passed and met by an incessant stream of officers and men in all kinds of costumes, on foot and mounted on every variety of charger; Zouaves were loitering about with baggy breeches, Turks with baggier.

A little way out is a booth with a flag floating over it—"Crimean Army Funds". It seemed to stand alone in its glory for no one went near it. Not so the general bazaar, in which a very brisk trade appears to go on in onions, soft soap, Dutch cheese, "English pasture excellent quality". Liquids of a stronger nature seemed to be staple commodities. Here we fell in with one of the 17th Light Dragoons who pointed out the scene of the famous cavalry charge. While musing upon this, up came some horses, led and mounted. "There", said he, "is our regiment." I counted them, thirteen in all. "You don't tell me that these are all?" "All that we can mount", he replied. These horses were a sad spectacle, rough, lanky, their heads down, their tails worn to the stumps, most of them showing great patches of bare skin. They seem to be too far gone to be brought round by the present fine weather and plentiful supply of forage. The horses of the French officers that I met are all still in good condition, sleek and fat. Soon came by a drove of mules ridden or led by Turks, Arabs, Maltese and Blackies, and concluded by a Highland lad half drunk, mounted on a mule, with toes stuck out and mouth reaching from ear to ear. He grinned out as he passed, "Here's the Royal Highland Brigade."

I saw no Russians, but on a hill beyond the Highland Corps of Sir Colin Campbell (Pl. 26) [Major-General Sir Colin Campbell, later Field-Marshal Lord Clyde, Commander of the Highland Division, had charge of the defences of the town and harbour of Balaclava] were a group of fellows squatting down on the ground in front of a little church, who were watching us in the valley and were pointed out to me as Russians. It is said there are 40,000 behind the hills and some more further up the valley. [Fenton refers to the Russian field army under the command of Prince Gortchakoff.]

Towards evening there were several reports of heavy guns over in the direction of Sebastopol, which made me very anxious to go and see what was the matter; no doubt I shall soon get used to them.

It is said that the people in the town to whom Lord Raglan has communicated the report of the Emperor's death do not believe it; others say that in consequence of it Mentchikoff has set off to St. Petersburg: you see to what a strait we are reduced for news here. [Shortly before the death of Nicholas I, Prince Mentchikoff was succeeded as Commander-in-Chief by Prince Michael Gortchakoff.]

I wish I had time to write you better descriptions of what I see around me, but to watch incessantly all that is going on, the frequent changes from the awful and grand to the intensely ridiculous, the constant succession of startling novelties, weary so much that I feel no energy to attempt a sufficient description of them. It is odder than three Bedlams broken loose. Don't lose any chance of writing; letters from home are more than meat and drink. Many kisses etc. etc. etc. from your model of a husband, R. F.

P.S. Friday morning [9th] 7 a.m. The dew fell so heavily last night that everything exposed to it was soaked. I think we shall have the horses disembarked this morning, and if so, I shall ride to camp. I am going to try to put them in the railway stables until my establishment is fitted up. At present I am fidgety and nervous, as I do not know whether all my boxes and apparatus will not have to stand by the waterside like many other heaps of things now here.

The wax and tape office to which one of our party is destined have been short of ink and have had to manufacture it of soot and vinegar.

8½ *a.m.* I am off, having so far done my duty to self and country by disposing of some salt fish and potatoes, eggs and buttered toast and tea. Good bye.

FIRST DAYS IN BALACLAVA

To William Agnew.

Balaclava, Friday 9th March

This morning I went on shore in good time, got a promise of stable room for a few days from the manager of the railways, also a place to store my boxes in till I can get them up to my permanent quarters. When I applied for rations for three horses Mr. Filder [the Commissary-General] asked me if I were a general's office! I shall get all I want with a little trouble, but these people must show their power or they would not be happy.

One serious omission I have made—the purchasing of a saddle and bridle. I have extracted a half-promise from Mr. Filder that I should be allowed to buy one from the Government stores, but on enquiry the storekeeper had gone. The railway people to my surprise have only two, which are in use.

Sparling, my A.D.C., went up last night to the quarters of the 4th Light Dragoons, to which regiment he formerly belonged, and tells me of a good site with plenty of water, close to the Commissariat Establishment and near Headquarters. He slept up in the camp last night and says there was heavy firing going on. I slept too well to hear it, though it was, I am told, very distinct down here. It was an attack on a new battery erected by the English close to the Russian works. I relied upon Sparling to get me a saddle from the regiment, but he has fallen on the back of his head through the sudden shoving off of a boat in which he went, and is so feverish now that I have thought it best to send for a doctor, who thinks his hurt rather serious.

Everything seems in much better order than "The Times" led me to expect. There are landing places of rough stones run out in several places, and store sheds are being put up. The main street is paved with broken stones with some sand thrown on it, and with a fortnight's traffic will be a good road. In the narrow passages between the houses may still be seen sufficient evidence of the state in which the roads were a month ago. The stench along the waterside is very bad, but they are taking pains to get rid of the filth. All the dead oxen and horses floating about the harbour have been towed out to sea. Do what they will, there is an immense quantity of putrefying matter which cannot be got rid of. The ground is everywhere thickly strewn with barley, the harbour is crammed with ships lying closer than in any docks, many of them empty, doing nothing themselves and keeping others from discharging their cargo.

There seems now no scarcity of carriage, at least there are quantities of fine mules, and many more coming. There is also plenty of forage, but the grain is most of it barley, and to the bad effect of this, more than to the exposure, the soldiers with whom I spoke attribute the great mortality among the horses.

Lord Raglan [Commander-in-the-Field of the British Army and Master-General of the Ordnance. The Commander-in-Chief of the Army was Lord Hardinge at Whitehall] was in town this morning with his staff. The soldiers have nothing but good words to say about him; one of them told me that when the weather was at the worst he was constantly sitting about amongst the men.

There are all sorts of rumours flying about, such as that tomorrow the grand attack is to begin. Yesterday we were told that the Emperor died of apoplexy, this morning it was pleurisy, and today it is the Empress.

Saturday [10th March]. This morning I had another hunt for saddles. After much trouble, Mr. Swan of the railway company promised that if I would lend him a horse, he would lend me a saddle and bridle. Sparling was unable to get out of bed and accompany me to the camp of the 4th Dragoons. We could not get the horses shod as the small nails were on board the "Candidete", not get-at-able, so we made the best of circumstances: awkward riding as ever I saw—railway sleepers, sheep, stones small and large, droves of mules with great saddles, artillery wagons, Commissariat stores and all sorts of odds and ends blocking the way.

About a mile out we turned in to the hillside, glad to get a little out of the throng, for the horses, being unbroken, made a row about everything. I now was made to feel how foolish I had been in omitting to buy a saddle, for in going up a stony rise the horse made a bound at something, burst the girth (there is but one), and in a moment I found myself with the saddle between my legs but no horse, down the hillside. I was much shaken, but got the saddle on again, fastened the girth to the other buckle, and rode on to the 4th Light Dragoons. Their quarter-master named Hill lent me a good saddle, and so we went across to the Kadikoi station. There is great activity with the railway workers; here a stationary engine is being erected to drag bricks up the hill where the road is at present steep, and huts are growing up very fast for the timekeeper and workmen. The magnificent cart horses belonging to the Company excite great admiration among the Turks.

I went on to Headquarters, and gave my letter for Lord Raglan to Lieut. Col. Steele [later General Sir Thomas Montague Steele, Lord Raglan's military secretary] who told me that if I could come back tomorrow at noon I could see his Lordship. Having explained to Col. Steele what my principal wants were, I was kindly directed by him to the place where I should find some of the gentlemen to whom I have letters. I found Mr. Angel, the Post Master General, who gave me a hearty welcome and promised to give me a hut in a week's time.

Leaving him I went across a little valley to Col. [later Sir John] Adye's (Royal Artillery), Lord Raglan's Adjutant. I need not say that I received from him the assurance of assistance in every possible way. As soon as I wish to leave Balaclava I am to give him notice and he will give me four strong horses to drag my carriage up the hill, for I have seen quite enough to be sure that my three could not do it, for they are light and would have to be broken in for draught. They will do very well on top. Col. Adye rode with me (after he had regaled me with ham and biscuits) part of the way back, and pointed out the positions of the various troops at Balaclava when the charge took place.

On reaching Balaclava I went to one of the railway surgeons, and had the satisfaction of hearing that no bones were broken and I shall be quit of pain in a few days. If I can get on horseback tomorrow I shall go to see Lord Raglan, but I scarcely think I shall be able, for I am badly shaken.

It is well I took the opportunity of getting horses at Gibraltar; I should otherwise have been comparatively helpless. I could have sold them many times over today, and met lots of people who are as much distressed for a horse as I was for a saddle.

I do not think if I could have seen all the difficulties of my task before setting out, that I should have had the courage to come. By pitching into them one by one I suppose they will be mastered.

DIFFICULTIES OF DISEMBARKATION

March 15th 1855.
Balaclava.

On Monday [12th] I set about getting my van ashore, had it hoisted up by pulleys from the mainyard and put upon its wheels, and while this was doing, went to see about a barge which had been promised to me by Captain Christie [the Harbour Master] the night before. I found the secretary and was told that the boats had all been sent out, but that I should have one the next day. Seeing that nothing was to be done in that direction I delivered several of my letters of introduction, and by evening was well tired out with running about from pillar to post. Hunting out anyone you want at Balaclava is good sport to a person not in a hurry, but if you want to make a find, it is vexation of spirit.

On Tuesday a small boat came to look at my carriage, for the secretary had been specially appealed to by Captain Anderson, to whom I had an introduction by Major Macgillwray [Ordnance Commissariat Officer], to whom (much better persuasion) I had introduced a bottle of porter. He (the said secretary) having looked at the van said I should want a barge, and for that, application must be made to the Admiral [Rear-Admiral Edward Boxer, second in command in the Mediterranean and Superintendent at Balaclava]. I met Captain Raymond, manager of the railway shipping. "Oh", said he, "why didn't you come to me? I'll manage it for you, you should always go to the proper people in these matters. You shall have a boat tomorrow; if I can't get to the ship's side I'll have the vessel shifted and put into the berth of yon red funnel steamer that leaves tonight." You must know that the ships here are packed as close as herrings in a barrel, and it is really hard to get anything heavy over the side.

Feeling somewhat relieved in mind, I resolved, nevertheless, to go to the Admiral, but on my way called at the ship on board of which lives [William] Simpson, who is sketching for Colnaghi. I found sitting in the cabin Captain Christie's secretary, so I asked him whether it was not extremely likely that

Admiral Boxer would refer me to Captain Christie and he to the individual before me. The probability of such an event being admitted, I then enquired as blandly as I could, to whom in that case I should be next referred. "To Captain Hamilton of the 'Drummond'" was the reply, "and he will supply you with a barge, and perhaps men to work it." "Then please give me a note to Captain Hamilton and I will try my luck with him." I had seen a lighter lying empty down the harbour and marked down its number, so when Captain Hamilton said he would willingly assist me but could not say when he should have a barge at liberty, I told him of this and he gave me permission to take it, giving me a note to the commander of the "Vesuvius". The officer there told me that the barge was ordered to take shot on board, but there was another lying alongside the next ship to ours, which was loading with shot, and when that was full, my carriage could be put on the top and so be carried ashore.

Back again I went to the "Hecla" and enquired of our neighbour when it was probable the barge would be loaded. "If I can get men, by tomorrow night", was the reply. This was encouraging. Having tried with these results the Government official assistance, I knew that I should most likely find Captain Raymond's promises of aid mere expressions of good will. I bethought me of Captain Barclay of the "Mohawk" transport (*Pl. 17*), who got my horses on shore, and whose boat I had not applied for through fear of its being too small and upsetting. He gave it to me in a minute, sent it round to the "Hecla", and in half an hour the carriage was on it, looking very top-heavy, it is true, but still able to retain its perpendicular, and being towed down the harbour was brought to a landing stage running from shore to the "Mohawk", and by pulleys from the yard-arm of the ship was hoisted upon the stage—a glorious example of the successful working of private enterprise.

I have given you the whole of this story just to show what a hunting up of people there is if one wants the simplest matter done here. In all my interviews I received the utmost attention and civility, and I believe that as much was done for me as the system would allow of, but it is *very* slow work. I am sure it would have taken a week before by Government aid I could have disembarked my van.

On Wednesday [14th], having set William and Sparling to clean glasses [for negatives], and getting everything ready for work next day, I got off on horseback to the camp with Captain Purdie. There is no need to amuse you with my sufferings for my country by aching of the ribs as I hobbled over the stones these three days, but this morning I have sufficiently recovered to get into the saddle without any lavish expenditure of expletives. I wanted an order for a hut in which to store my heavy boxes at Balaclava, so that I might take up to the camp nothing more than was immediately wanted. This I could only get from Headquarters. Colonel Hill introduced me to General Airey [General Sir James Talbot Airey, Quartermaster-General] who gave me a letter to Captain Reeve at Balaclava containing the necessary order, also a letter to Sir Colin Campbell. I did not see Lord Raglan, who was unwell.

Having been hospitably entertained by an A.D.C. of General Airey's and received my letters, I thought of enquiring for letters and papers sent up to the post office for me, but on enquiry was told they must be at Balaclava. Prepared by previous experience to apply elsewhere, I was only moderately disgusted, the more so as I had previously taken my revenge on Angel the P.M. by approaching him under the guise of friendship, enquiring about the state of his health, and conversing about the weather, friends at home and things in general, until he was reduced to a state of unsuspicious confidence, when I suddenly stabbed him with the question, "Well, Angel, when do you expect the next mail?". "D—— the mail!" was the answer.

Having a good part of the day before me, I rode on towards the front and enquired for General Barnard [Lieut.-General (Sir) Henry William Barnard, Grenadier Guards (Pl. 60)] to whom Mr. Angel gave me an introduction. His tent is pitched on a slope looking down towards the town [Sebastopol], a beautiful situation. He was at lunch with another officer and made me join in, some more bacon was fried and another bottle of porter discharged its cork against the Russian batteries and we refreshed the inner man, watching the puffs of smoke as the batteries on either side discharged occasionally at each other. Afterwards he got on horseback and rode with us to the picket house, a hut on a hill commanding a fine view of the town.

The Malakoff was just in front, and from the earthworks there were coming balls into one of our batteries a little to the right down the hill, which again was firing shells at a battery the Russians are making on the Garden Hill, the same the French were driven from some nights since with loss. I could see the shells from our guns go right into the Russian works, and was much surprised at the accuracy of the firing at objects such a distance away.

Thence we rode to Lieut. General Sir Richard England's quarters [in command of the third Division]. I was introduced to him, and after some chat he joined us and volunteered to show us St. George's Monastery. Sir Richard may be a bad soldier but he is not a bad rider, for he led us across a pretty country for delicate nerves: steep ascents of bare rock just sprinkled with a little earth, marshy hollows with a sluggish stream in the middle, vineyards with stumps sticking a few inches out of the ground, and rugged uplands, all jagged with rock and loose stones. Having some miles to go [six miles], the pace was stiff. This, and the jolts *and* the jumps tried my damaged rib sorely, but the view at the Monastery was well worth the trouble: a quiet sunny nook perched upon a platform of rock beneath the crest of a hill, the blue sea far, far down, lazily crisping its margin against the base of huge fantastic rocks; halfway down, patches of olives and evergreens wherever a little earth had gathered. A few Russian peasants loitering about, a monk or two moving silently on to join in the evening service—these formed a picture of dreamy repose, which was only heightened by the contrast of a dashing Zouave clad in a garb of many colours. When service began we entered the little chapel which has been used by the monks since the storm of the 14th November, which so shook their church that the doors have got jammed. The same storm has turned up the edges of the copper roof, which would be stripped off (if not repaired) by another such storm. In such an out-of-the-way place the service, of course, is very simple compared with that of the great convent of Kiev, but I enjoyed it much, as it brought before me again impressions which I never expected to receive but from memory or dreams. [Fenton refers to his journey to Russia in 1852.]

Leaving this place we parted from the two generals after I had received from General Barnard an invite to repeat my visit and a promise of a bed in his tent whenever I liked to sleep up at the front.

On our way back we passed a little level space about half a mile across where there had just been taking place "The Great Crimean Hurdle Races". At the top of the hill before beginning the descent we stopped to look at the valley of Balaclava spread out like a map beneath our feet, the heights round the harbour dotted with tents looking like molehills.

A day or two back, while getting down the ship's side my famous knife dropped into the water. Having duly lamented its loss I considered it "Down among the dead men" and grew resigned. On my return this night it was put into my hand very little the worse for its aquatic excursion. On our vessel there are four divers who came out with us. They wanted to try their apparatus, so went down at the place where I dropped the knife, the water being about twenty feet in depth. It was found in ten minutes, and another one besides. They say the bottom of the harbour is covered with beef bones thrown out of the ships. They had been thrice down to the wreck of the "Prince" [sunk in the hurricane of 14–15th November 1854]. The hull of the ship, and that of a wooden vessel sunk near, is torn about as if pounded in a mortar. Today they came upon a quantity of saddles all rotten, and after a little search they found a great quantity of dead bodies, their clothing all washed away by the water. Few of the bodies were entire, being mangled and disjointed by the wreck grinding about them: what a horrible sight! The men seem to shrink from speaking of it.

Presenting my order to Captain Reeve for a hut, I was assured that if I would call again next week I should have one, but that there were none taken upon shore yet. I could not content myself with such an answer, and upon further enquiry found that there were already two huts on shore, appropriated but not called for in a hurry by their owners. I got one of these, which was labelled for General Barnard. Thence I went to Colonel Harding, Governor of Balaclava, to ask him for a site to erect it and he gave me one at once, a very good spot in the rear of his own quarters. He is the only officer who did not tell me that I could have what I wanted in two or three days!

The hut was up at the end of the harbour on the other side, so I had to go and borrow a boat and a couple of hands to get it across. Colonel Harding gave me a gang of Croats to level the ground; I set them to work with an English soldier to keep them at it. On my return with the boat they had all disappeared. [*Croats is a misnomer. These hired labourers were Asiatic subjects of the Sultan, but in camp language were described as "Croats" because they happened to arrive at a time when some men from Croatia were expected.*] It could not be helped, so I went with the boatmen, set them to work transporting the hut in pieces to its destination, and returned to my van where I had left Sparling and William preparing for work.

BEGINNING OF PHOTOGRAPHIC WORK

I took a few pictures, beginning with Her Majesty's post office. Here began troubles of a new character. In order to avoid the necessity of explaining to all comers what my carriage was for, I had made Sparling paint on it "Photographic Van". While developing a picture, a conversation went on outside which I give as a specimen of many similar ones: "Eh, Jem, what's that, P.H.O. to graph. Is that anything to do with the [telegraph] line?" "No, they say there's a chap in there taking pictures." "Is there? Then he shall take mine." A knock at the door and a good pull to open it without waiting for an answer. The door being locked, there was another knock and another speech: "Here you fellow, open the door and take my picture." The door was opened and he was told that we were not taking portraits. "What did you come for if you're not going to take pictures? I'll have mine done, cost what it may. What's to pay?" "It can't be done now, pay or no pay." "Can't it, though? I'll go to Mr. Beatty and get an order for it; I'll have it, and I'd like to see the man that'll stop me, *you* won't, nor Lord Raglan himself." Many of these interruptions are very droll, but they *are* still interruptions.

Friday [*16th March*]. Got the carpenter from the ship to work at my hut. Received a notice that the stables where my horses were, were wanted for the railway mules and that I must have them out that day; having no place to put them in, decided to take no notice of the intimation. I find William almost useless to me; if I speak to him he stares and says, "Sure, I do my best, sir."

There are all kinds of internal wars going on here, between the Admiral and the railway, and between the naval officers and the transport captains engaged by the railway company. The naval management of the railway does not seem at all good. The ships do not get unloaded and the Admiral has been obliged to order some of them away.

After running about in the morning, I took a few pictures after twelve, but not very successful ones, as my van is in the midst of all the dust and turmoil of the railway yard (*Pl. 22*), and as I have too much anxiety about preliminary arrangements to be able to work to any purpose.

I have lots of invitations from the camp to go and stay with them, but have really too much bother to accept them at present.

Today I got out the quietest of my three nags, harnessed him, and went to get the loan of a small cart to train him to draught with Major MacGillwray of the Artillery, who gave me leave to take one of their carts and put the horse to it. He went on very well while leading him, and for a while after one of the soldiers got into the cart and drove, but happening to step upon a broken bottle he kicked out, threw his leg over the shaft and came down, breaking the harness to pieces. Not having come to train horses, and seeing that without any facility for breaking them in and without any clear spaces for them to jump about, it would take me a long time to get them fit for draught, I got rather dismal and sent the horse back to the stable, and thought with Solomon that all things were vanity and vexation of spirit.

Thereupon I resolved to try some other plan, so went to Major Anderson, and by his advice wrote a demand for a couple of draught horses or mules to the Colonel commanding, and wrote also to Colonel Adye begging him to back the demand. Having done this I went to Mr. [James] Beatty, chief engineer of the railway, and made the same request to him during my stay down here. He acceded at once, telling me that on giving notice the night before they were wanted, I should have horses.

There, I have given you a brief sketch of all my labours, sorrows and pleasures down to this present. It is a very imperfect sketch of both; such as it is, however, you must take care of it for me to read when I get home as I have too much to do to be able to appreciate properly what I am seeing and hearing.

When with General Barnard the other day he told me that a Polish officer of rank had come over to them, and read me the information obtained from him. It was "that there are 50,000 men in Sebastopol with plenty to eat but short of spirit, worn out with work, but quite ready to fight; that they had plenty of ammunition, for their communications were all open, that they would fight for the new Emperor as for the old, that the Poles were all anxious to desert but were closely watched. The soldiers all swore allegiance to Alexander the day before." [Alexander II who succeeded Nicholas I.]

The same night there was heavy firing. I sat on deck smoking a cigar and watched the flashes for about half an hour; the sky was continually lit up with the red glare, there seemed to be 80 or 90 shots per minute. Altogether the firing lasted about two hours with much violence. There was an attack of some kind, but by whom or with what results I could not learn, for there were fifty different stories. I heard the most opposite stories from the men actually engaged. The French soldiers seem to be getting into disrepute in our army as wanting in pluck. This is a strange character to give them, but everyone says the same thing about them. They were beaten back by the Russians in their attempt to take the Garden battery, and I am told the other night they ran away through the midst of our working parties. This may be all scandal and very likely is; I tell it as it was told to me.

I have got my portmanteau at last, but it is not the fashion to wear shirts here. There is no such institution as a washerwoman; those who can, send their linen to Malta to be washed! I have bought a Guernsey shirt from Mr. Lean, from a vessel sent out by the Earl of Eglinton to sell things at cost price, and found that I could have got the same quality cheaper from one of the regular dealers. Whatever the intentions of the senders of the ships, somebody is making a very large profit out of the articles contained in them.

AT THE GUARDS' CAMP

Balaclava, March 28th.

I have got some jolly pictures of Balaclava with my big lenses, having given up working the small cameras until I receive my Ross lenses. Two days ago I went up to the Generals' camp [Sir Colin Campbell's and General Cameron's] outside Balaclava, between here and Kadikoi. Captain Holder [Fusilier Guards] invited me and promised to get me a dark-room contrived if I would take the view from the Camp, so I put up my camera &c. on a pack saddle on one of my horses and went there.

On going up to the Guards I made the acquaintance of Lord Rokeby [later Lieut.-General, in command of the 1st Division], to whom I gave the parcel entrusted to my care. He introduced me to Colonel de Ballie, a young man about my own age, who was busy putting a padlock on a fowl house he had just constructed, grumbling away all the time at the Crimea, at the army, and at his own particular hardships. He made me a very liberal offer of his commission, medals, and other advantages, if I would only get him safe back to Pall Mall. He had just got up a Maltese hut and has papered it with prints cut out of the 'Illustrated London News'. They are getting quite a farmyard at the Guards' camp, sheep with lambs following them, turkeys, geese and chickens are abundant.

I dined with Captain Holder, Colonel Manson—half-brother of your mother's cousin—being the only guest; had gravy soup, fresh fish caught in the bay, liver and bacon fried, a shoulder of mutton, pancakes with quince preserve, cheese, stout, sherry and cigars.

At 10.30 p.m. I made my first essay at camp life. It was windy but I slept well till 4.30 when cocks and hens, sheep and lambs, began their morning hymns. Then the Turks in the valley below began to make an awful noise which they supposed to be music; shortly after, the different bands of the Guards struck up, and the row was so great that sleep was impossible. At seven, Captain Holder's servant brought me a cup of chocolate and I got up and went to the top of the hill and strolled about till nine, when we breakfasted on potted tongue, tea, toast, fish and marmalade.

Colonel Seymour [Fusilier Guards] promised to let me have his tent, which is a double one and very dark, to work in, and when he had turned out (which was not before 10.30) we set to work to fit it up, succeeded after an hour's work, and took a picture. When I came to develop it I found that the tent was not light-proof, so went with all my traps further up the hill to a hut where the owner was away. Here Sparling and I made a capital place, but just as all was ready the wind, which had been freshening, became a gale, the sky darkened, the tents were stretching and straining as if they would burst, and matters looked hopeless. I waited some hours, and tried four times to take pictures when a gleam of light burst out. I succeeded once, but as the storm increased, gave it up.

In Colonel Seymour's tent my bed had been set up and I turned in and in spite of the storm slept soundly till four, when I awoke and found my tent making convulsive starts, leaping from the ground and shivering down again. On peeping through the doorway, the whole camp seemed to be alive though no one was about, for the tents were making strange contortions in the moonlight. Inside, my coverlet was lifted up by every gust, I could not wrap it round me so that the wind would be kept out, and so I lay trying to calculate the direction in which the tent would fall when the crash came, and having found my head was to leeward, was kept in a state of watchful suspense. A few tents were blown down and a good many huts. There was nothing to be done but print, so I went down to Balaclava and set to work at that, and as the prints came out of the frames there was soon an admiring crowd around us: it becomes a great bore because one must give a civil answer to everyone.

Colonel Harding came and told me to ask him for everything that I might want to complete my establishment here. I shall soon try him, for there is always something wanting. I dined with him in the evening in a house formerly occupied by the Russian commandant of the town. I had a very agreeable evening.

A MIDNIGHT BATTLE

There have been for the last fortnight a succession of fierce encounters at night, principally between the French and Russians for the possession of some rifle pits which annoy our lines very much. The French have repeatedly taken them, but are regularly driven out again with great loss. The Zouaves get on well but are not properly supported by the other French troops. The night before last [22nd March] there was an awful row. [Sortie from the Malakoff.] It seems that there was first a fight between the Russians and French in which the latter were hard pressed, that the English went to help them, and that while our men were thus occupied the Russians attacked our trenches, overpowered the men left in them, and held them for twenty minutes till driven out. The loss was great on both sides.

On the night of 22nd March four large-scale Russian sorties were made with the object of checking the advance to the Mamelon of the approaches which the French were constructing. The 5,500 Russians were eventually driven back by the French and English in what almost amounted to a midnight battle. The Russians lost 1,300 dead and wounded, the French 600 and the British 70.

The bodies lay unburied all the next day; two men from our ship were up there and saw them lying in heaps, the Russians and French in lines with their feet almost touching. One Zouave was lying by himself almost in the Russian batteries.

Yesterday there was a truce to bury them and the officers of the two armies met and chatted. An officer of the Guards who was present told me that the Russian officers chaffed ours, asking them when our army was going away. This was an unusually hot affair, but it is going on in this way nearly every night without any result to either party, except that the Russians have maintained the positions to which they advanced a short time since, and that the French are sinking in general opinion as wanting pluck. I do not think that Sebastopol will ever be taken till the north side is invested. Most people say it never will be taken at all.

The soldiers seem very comfortable and look in splendid condition. Now that the railway is at work they have not nearly so much to do. The daily supplies needed at the camp amount to 112 tons weight and used to require nearly 2,000 horses to convey it. This and a great deal more is now done by rail.

Monday [26th March]. I heard today that at the time of the truce a Russian officer told ours that the Lancaster gun was doing them a great deal of mischief, but said "Wait until tomorrow morning and you'll see something." The morning came and with it the fire of a 63-pounder from the Mamelon battery. The news was telegraphed up to Headquarters with an enquiry of what was to be done. The answer was, "Fight it", so at it they went, and instead of shell loaded the guns with round shot: the first discharge hit the Russian gun in the muzzle and splintered it to pieces.

In the afternoon I was up at the Generals' [Sir Colin Campbell and General Cameron] to take the splendid view from their camp. It was very windy and several pictures were spoilt. The wind was a sirocco, thermometer 82° in the shade; my camera slides in one hour's work warped and split with the dry heat. Afterwards I dined with my former host (Captain Holder), Colonel Manson and Captain Hilder: soup, fish, cutlets, boiled turkey, rice pudding and preserves. While smoking, we were alarmed by a succession of shots on the slope of the hill below. Half an hour later I left them, and in walking down the hill came upon the whole body of Croats [labourers] drawn up in two lines, at the end of which I found a picket of guards, who told me that the firing must have been among these men, who were now under arrest. Six of them were lying dead on the ground. Life seems to be squandered here like everything else. Among the prisoners was an old man whose portrait I took the other day. They will be tried tomorrow and probably some shot, others flogged, and the whole disarmed. However much this may impair their picturesque looks, this is a very necessary step as they are armed up to the teeth, and you will see by their portraits not mild-mannered men (*Pl. 36*).

I get on very slowly with my work here; the labour in itself is great, and many pictures are spoilt by the dust and heat, still more by the crowds of all ranks who flock round. I am afraid I shall not get away as soon as I expected. I dread the hot weather and shall do my best to get away before it comes, but the distances are so great and the difficulty of getting the people together whose portraits are wanted, that it will take me much time. I send you a portrait of some Croats: let Dr. Becker [Prince Albert's secretary, Queen Victoria's librarian, and tutor to the Princes] (*Pl. 5*) see it, and take care no publisher sees it.

Could I *write what I see as I see* it, my letters would be very amusing, but it is stupid work writing when the excitement of the day is over and one's eyes are heavy. I do not, however, forget to indulge in a little quiet meditation about home and its dear inhabitants, even when too tired to write.

April 4th, 1855.

I am still at Balaclava, partly because there is so much to be done here, and partly because while I live on board ship there is no need to waste time in cooking.

This last week I have been travelling about with the van in the Guards' and Cavalry camp (*Pl. 32*), getting some interesting views, with a few portraits of "great guns". Everybody is bothering me for their portrait to send home; were I to listen to them and take the portrait of all comers I should be busy from now to Christmas and might make a regular gold digging in the Crimea, but I am very anxious to get up to the front. I have been up twice to see about a site and look for points of view. It is no easy work even on horseback: the distances are so great and the ravines so numerous, that it takes the best part of the day to go round the English and French lines of attack.

After taking a picture from the top of the Guards' Hill, I wanted to get a negative of the little hills whence the Turkish troops were driven on the 25th October [Battle of Balaclava]. Having received an invitation from the Colonel of Sparling's regiment, from whose camp there is a good view of the position, I got a couple of railway horses and moved up there. After taking the views, the foreground of which was formed by the camp of the 4th Light, the officers got their winter dresses out and I made up some interesting groups of them (*Pl. 71*).

A FIRE AT BALACLAVA

Last night there was an alarm. On reaching the deck I saw a great volume of flame and smoke close beside us. At first it seemed to be the next ship but was really on shore, about twenty yards from our store. The wind was blowing down the town, and I really thought everything would be destroyed. There was a cry for the ship's bucket, and very soon the street, which ten minutes before was as still as death, was crowded with men shouting in all languages, everyone giving orders, no one obeying. A number of buckets were soon there, and some kind of order was got. Some tore down the surrounding sheds, others climbed upon the top of the burning buildings and emptied the buckets there, but the fire gained ground rapidly until the engines came, four of which at last subdued it. It was a narrow escape. When all was over, up came the sappers and began making energetic preparations for extinguishing it, commencing by clearing the ground of those who had rendered their aid needless—much to the amusement of most, and the indignation of a few, of the excluded.

In the morning I was up at the camp, called on Captain Wilkinson and got him to take me to see the best views of the town [Sebastopol]. From his tent we walked along for half a mile, coming towards the end upon Russian cannon balls scattered about. Further on the balls lay thicker, but in coming to a ravine called "the Valley of Death" the sight passed all imagination: round shot and shell lay like a stream at the bottom of the hollow all the way down, you could not walk without treading upon them. Following the course of the ravine towards the town we came to a cavern in which some soldiers were stationed as a picket. They had made a garden in front, forming the borders of the beds with cannon balls. We had gone a little further down and were admiring the rugged outline of the rock and pointing out where the face had been smashed by the Russian fire, when we were startled by a great crack in the rock in front of us and a cloud of dust, followed by a second knock upon the opposite face of the ravine as the ball bounded across it, and then a heap of stones and the ball rolled away together down the ravine. Further progress in this direction was voted inadvisable.

Before getting to this glen we had been to an elevation just behind one of our batteries called Strong Hill, were prevented by the sentries from mounting it, but making a flank march got to the front of it, and lying down behind some stones, had a good look into the Russian batteries and saw some very neat shell practice from our battery into the Mamelon and some ditto from the Russians against our English battery, to which we were going next. Crossing a ravine down which the Woronzoff Road [from Prince Woronzoff's estate at Yalta to Inkerman, thence to Sebastopol, but made impassable by Russian fire] runs into the town, the roadway was ploughed up in several places, the earth showing that it had just been turned up. On the hill-top for half a mile in the rear of the battery at which the Russians were firing, the path of their balls of that day's firing was marked by a regular succession of furrows. General Barnard's tent, at which I was invited to sleep whenever I went to camp, was towards the end of the range of this fire, and a night or two since, while he was in bed, a ball came in and broke the leg of his table, another made mutton of a sheep nearby, so he has been obliged to move.

I had a roll that day over Hecla's head. I am very sorry to say that though the admiration of everybody for his spirit and beauty, he is not safe upon his pins, and I have been for some time expecting what happened yesterday: trotting down a bit of a hill, rather smooth and gravelly, he fell and shot me over his head. I have an impression that I made a somersault in the air. Anyhow, it was a very clean fly out of the saddle; he was none the worse nor I, but we both might have been, so I mean to sell him. It is a pity, for he will follow me like a dog, gallops and jumps beautifully—the latter a very valuable quality here.

Every day the last week has been named for the commencement of the grand attack. It is certainly to be soon, for the ships that are capable of containing invalids have received orders to be ready to start. Shot and powder and heavy guns have been going up to the front in great quantities, and today a large number of stretchers for the wounded have gone up. I go up tomorrow, but shall be two or three days on the road as I have to call at the Artillery Camp and the Heavy Cavalry, and at the Kadikoi Hill. This morning I have been printing, and have taken a few portraits, amongst others that of Prince Edward of Saxe Weimar [Lieut.-Colonel, Grenadier Guards].

While up at the Guards the other day, the guests at dinner were all attired in what we call the Balaclava livery, a grey coat lined inside with fur, very light and comfortable and of no particular shape. I happened to say that I should like to be inside one of them as lawful owner thereof so that I might come out strong as a Crimean hero. Today there came to my hut one of the party with one of these coats which he handed to me, the only drawback to my pleasure in receiving it being that the said gentleman had the night before informed me that it was thickly populated. I have been in terror ever since of being crawled away with. As a precaution I have got my hair cut close by the barber of the 4th Light, and have bargained with one of the ladies here [presumably a soldier's wife or camp follower] for a wash of my clothes at 6d. a piece. You would be amused with the conceit put on by everyone that sports a petticoat here; people look at the wearers as if they were some strange natural curiosity, the washerwomen toss their heads and give themselves airs.

Mr. Newlands of Liverpool, who has come to look after the sanitary arrangements, breakfasted with me this morning. He says he can make this place as healthy as any English town if allowed. He is going to make a slaughter house at the entrance of the harbour and have all the offal carried out four miles to sea; at present eighty sheep are slaughtered every day in the vessels in harbour alone and the entrails thrown into the water alongside. All over the camp the animals wanted for food are killed close to the tents and the parts not used are rotting for days. I never ride out without finding dead horses, even right away on the top of the hills. It is a great treat after the day's work is over to get on to the hill and enjoy the pure air after inhaling all day the depressing atmosphere of Balaclava. There are several places where one can get a gallop for half a mile over pretty level ground, and a regular raceground has been marked out. There are races in some part of the camp at least twice a week; now that there is little doing and the soldiers and officers are comfortable, they want something to keep them from stagnating. Next Saturday there are races at the 88th. Two of the officers lunched here today and invited us all to go up.

Wednesday [4th April]. There has been very heavy firing today, but the promised opening of all the batteries did not take place. It is now said to be adjourned until the question of peace or war is finally settled; up to the present time the Russians have decidedly the best of it, that is the siege, though whenever they attack they lose heaps of men, but they keep advancing their works and getting fresh batteries made and new rifle pits. Wray of the 88th told me that two nights since, when he was in the trenches, a sentry came and reported that the Russians had a large body of men and two guns outside their works as if going to attack. They (the 88th) got their support under arms and waited. All night they saw these troops, but there was no attack. Next morning they found a new rifle pit dug close to their trenches: how the Russians must have laughed at the gallant 88th! Next night there was an attempt to repeat the same manoeuvre, but when the evening brought out their troops the 88th fired at them, and next morning there was no new rifle pit dug.

PROGRESS TO HEADQUARTERS

I have commenced my march today [4th April]. The van is about a mile out of Balaclava at the quarters of the 71st (*Pl. 30*). It is time to move, for the whole place is one great *pigsty*. It is astonishing to me how little I have done now that I have been here a month, and yet I have been working hard all the time. My hut seems to be the rendezvous of all the Colonels and Captains in the army, everybody drops in every day, and I can scarcely get time to work for questions. I wish you could do a little of it for me, even if only to clear the hut of visitors you could be useful, for when I scold William for letting any one in he says, "Sure I tell them, but they don't mind".

To William Agnew

April 9th 1855.

I send by this day's post a few views and portraits. It is so difficult to print pictures here, especially the large ones, that I send what I have got, whether toned or not. About a fortnight since, I sent off a parcel by Mr. Smith, one of the Post Masters here, who was going down to Constantinople. He was to show them to Lord Stratford and send them on from there. I have got about three times as many as what I have sent, but have had no time to print them. Lord [later General] George Paget and General Scarlett [Lieut.-General Sir James Yorke Scarlett] I think I have sent you.

My van is now halfway up to H.Q., and had today been fine would have arrived there. I have been, after establishing myself at Balaclava, working my way up, taking pictures of remarkable sights and persons, so that I may not have to return here except to embark. Sir Colin Campbell I have not yet got; he is up at four every morning and either writing and not to be disturbed, or scampering about.

Yesterday I was up at H.Q. and got a site given me on which to erect my tent. I shall have some days' work up here before I can do much; I have to get up my tent, build a stable, and another hut if I can get the order for one, make a kitchen and find a cook, the latter is the greatest bother. If possible I shall get one of Lord Raglan's bodyguard; as I can make out a case of necessity I think the application will be attended to. Our time is so completely occupied with work that there is no chance of our getting anything to eat if we have to look after it ourselves.

I have never touched my colours yet; I must devote some days to sketching when everything else is finished. There are a few good sketches in the camp which I shall try to get, but generally the officers who are at the front are too hard worked to have time for sketching. [William] Simpson (*Pl. 40*) who is working for Colnaghi, makes only pencil outlines on the ground and puts in the colour from memory. [Edward] Goodall [line-engraver] who is here for the "Illustrated London News", has been ill, not doing much. His sketches which appear in the paper seem to astonish everyone from their total want of likeness to the reality, and it is not surprising that it should be so, since you will see from the prints sent herewith that the scenes we have here are not bits of artistic effect which can be effectually rendered by a rough sketch, but wide stretches of open country covered with an infinity of detail.

I have found a much better way of getting my van conveyed to the site I select than by applying to the authorities. As soon as a few of the prints had been seen, I was overwhelmed with applications to go here and there to take a portrait or a view of some tent or camp. If it is a place where I want to go, I go if they will drag the van up, and if it does not take me out of my way to Headquarters. For any very heavy pull the Artillery give me six horses for small distances; the men turn out in the hope of getting photographed in a group. This way I have travelled during the past week a great part of the way up, and had it not been pouring with rain I should have got there this evening. All the heavy part of my baggage not immediately needed I leave in my hut down here [Balaclava] where I print; the rest will be sent up by one of the railway wagons to the top of the hill and I shall have to cart it from there if I can borrow a cart, or carry it piecemeal on my horses by pack saddle.

Today is the first wet day we have had, and the croakers say that now it has begun it will last a fortnight. The streets in Balaclava are already almost impassable. Water was much needed, for the wells were drying up and the earth baked hard as a stone. In the valley round Balaclava there is not a blade of anything green to rest the eyes upon, but on the hill-tops and away from the neighbourhood of the troops the ground has been sprinkled with crocuses and snowdrops and now it is covered with the purple and yellow iris, with primroses and other flowers unknown to me. Though my horses will not draw the van, I find them exceedingly useful, as the distances are so great that without them so much of our time and bodily strength would be wasted in mere locomotion. It will take me longer than I calculated to get through my work here. I shall write to the British Museum to get them to defer, if possible, the commencement of this year's photographic work.

I shall be glad to have a letter from you to say what you think of the prints. If you have not got a portrait of Lord Cardigan I should recommend you to take no trouble about it, as you will before long have a very different account of his conduct from that he has himself given. I have heard men and officers in the Cavalry regiments discussing his conduct and not one has a good word to say for him. He is said to have been twenty minutes *before any one else out of the action at Balaclava.* Lord Lucan is no great favourite, but the officers all sympathize with him and say he is badly used and that he had no chance but to act as he did. Please remember that this letter is not intended for everybody to see generally, it would be very injurious to me were any of my letters to get into the papers.

The report has been circulated all last week that the fire was to open from all the batteries today at five in the morning. Such reports have been so common that we do not know what to believe, but if one can believe one's own ears it is this time true for ever since I was up we have heard guns firing up in front about 10 to 15 shots a minute. It is said that the bombardment is to last five days and that then the troops are to storm. If they do no more than dismount the Russian guns I shall be able to take my van down to the batteries: at present it would be smashed in two minutes after it was seen on the top of the hill.

THE SECOND BOMBARDMENT OF SEBASTOPOL

The long-planned bombardment of Sebastopol which started on 9th April was intended to damage the forts defending the town and open up the way for an assault. In the ten days of this April bombardment the Russians lost 6,131 killed and wounded. Every night they repaired their defences and brought them into a state for fighting again when morning broke.

April 19th 1855.

The attack on the town commenced on Monday [9th April] in the midst of a storm of heavy rain and wind. I intended to have been at Headquarters by Monday evening but when I went ashore in the morning the streets were a regular quagmire and the rain pouring down in such torrents, that I saw it would be useless to attempt moving the van, so knowing nothing better to do, I resolved to go up and see the row in front. I got on my black horse, put on my long boots for the first time, and that wonderful waterproof cap, and set off.

On the top of the hill where the camp is, the driving mist was so thick that I lost my way and should not easily have found it again without the aid of the firing, which told me in which direction I ought to go. We had heard from five in the morning the constant firing of heavy guns: the sound was deadened by the mist and rain, and it was at first doubtful whether the bombardment had actually begun. However, there was no mistake about it as I got near. Unfortunately it was so thick that we could scarcely see more than the puffs of smoke from our own batteries; of the Russian batteries I could see only indications through the mist. All day the two parties had been firing almost by guesswork. It was getting dark so I went straight to the 88th, found Wray in his tent with Colonel Maxwell and joined them in discussing a game pie just arrived from Ireland.

Leaving Wray I went off to Hallewell's tent as I wished to spend the night with him, and roused his servant, who on hearing my name said, "Oh! Sir, Master has been expecting you a long time, he said that if you came I was to make you comfortable." Recommending him to obey his master's orders to the letter, while he went off to tell Hallewell (*Pl. 44*), who was dining close by with General Brown [Lieut.-General Sir George Brown, Commander of the Light Division] I managed very well with a bottle of champagne and ditto of whisky and a box of cigars. Having arranged all this I sat cosily, now and then stretching my head out of the tent to look at the shells as they wobbled about in the sky. Once a double shell (two chemicals together) came from the Russians: they formed a beautiful exhibition of fireworks, especially when they burst just before touching the ground. When Hallewell came in with his "I say, how do you do, old boy" I was in a comfortable state, wishing happiness to everybody in general and the present company in particular. He being like-minded, we had a very pleasant evening talking of absent friends, and Hallewell became enthusiastic about his recollections of my studio, and our *tête à tête* lasted till 1 a.m.

Next morning early I set off by myself to Cathcart's Hill (*Pl. 48*) [the burial ground of Lieut.-General Sir George Cathcart, Commander of the 4th Division, and many other officers who fell at Inkerman] the best spot for a general view of Sebastopol. It seemed so far from the town that I was afraid I could not see anything from the hill, and therefore climbed down towards Chapman's Battery, which is halfway between Cathcart's Hill and the town, rather nearer though. The Russians fired constantly. I thought I should have got a good sight here but found that I must go farther, so went down the hollow of the hill, looking sharp out, for the ground here is covered with cannon balls, and I took care to keep well behind the hill in going down, for I could hear by the whir and thud that the balls were coming up the ravine on each side. When I had got so far, the row was so great I felt quite stunned and dare not go to the top of the hill. There was no stop to the awful commotion in the air. The 68-pounders especially almost burst the ears, and the shot from them sounded like an express train that had broken off the line and leapt up into the air. The shot and shell did not disturb me so much as the awful clangour, as if all hell had broken loose and the legions of Lucifer were fighting in the air. I could only see the Russian redoubt indistinctly, the mist was so thick and the smoke hung heavily, but it was easy to see that they were not firing one gun to our four. It must have been uncomfortable in their quarters. Seeing that I was afraid, I thought it best to walk backwards so that I could see if any shot were coming.

At breakfast Hallewell told me that in the previous day's fire the Russians appeared to have suffered little and that in the English batteries only five men were killed and seven wounded. He seemed to have small expectations of a successful result, and I find this is the general opinion. As it is still raining and foggy and nothing visible of the effects of the fire, I set off home. Hallewell showed me first a panorama of the town and country which he had made for the Queen; it is very good indeed and has been much admired in the camp. Sir John Campbell told me that if he were ever at the head of an army Hallewell should be his Quartermaster-General. I hear his praise in everyone's mouth.

All that week the bombardment continued; we heard it at Balaclava faint or loud according to the wind, and all sorts of rumours flew about: that we were to be attacked tonight, that the Russians had sent out a flag of truce and wished to surrender, that the fleet was to go in, that it had been in and blown up Fort Constantine, that the Russian batteries were ground to powder, that one of ours was all destroyed, and a score of others equally founded on fact. Meanwhile I was printing and making preparations for going up to Headquarters, sending up my boxes by rail and looking for a site for my tent.

On Friday [13th April] I pitched my tent and got many of my things arranged there. The Artillery had lent me six horses to drag the van up the hill. At the railway depot at the top I took up as many boxes as the springs of the carriage could bear.

ARRIVAL OF THE TURKISH ARMY

When the tent was pitched I went to present a letter I had written to Lord Raglan asking for a soldier as servant, and whilst there, there came a sound of strange music anything but harmonious from the other side of a small valley. We saw it was the vanguard of Omar Pasha's army, which had just landed at Kamiesch Bay [the French port, from Eupatoria]. They went past in good order by batallions and regiments, the staff at the head of the first regiment, which had a band playing European music with moderate success. The men were fine athletic fellows, well dressed and armed. As they came up to where we were all standing, each band struck up, and sometimes the strain was so ludicrous that it was greeted with a general smile. It was very beautiful to see them rounding up the hillside, to see column after column appearing on the ridge, their bayonets flashing in the light, and the officers prancing past on showily caparisoned Arabian horses. The artillery went along the road below, and in very good state it seemed. Altogether about 18,000 men passed, and then there came a host of baggage horses and stragglers. They made a very favourable impression on everyone. On going home at night their tents were whitening the hills on the ridge overlooking Balaclava and their sentries replaced the French along the lines of defence in this part.

> *Omar Pasha's army of 40,000 was at Eupatoria, north of Sebastopol. At the request of General Canrobert, the French Commander-in-Chief, and with the unwilling acquiescence of Lord Raglan, Omar Pasha came with a contingent of 15 to 18,000 men for a limited period to the already overcrowded seat of war before Sebastopol.*

Next day 9,000 went past but this lot were Egyptian and all coffee-coloured. These were also fine men. [Under the command of Ismael Pasha, later Khedive of Egypt.]

Finding I could get no answer to my application about a servant, I resolved to go at once to the front and take Sebastopol—by photography. Colonel Adye got me horses and I took the van to the rear of Cathcart's Hill to be out of sight of the Russians—not that there is any danger of their hitting it, but it might draw their fire and so somebody in the neighbourhood get hit. On the way I met General Barnard who asked me to dine with him the next day.

LIFE AT THE CAMP BEFORE SEBASTOPOL

At Cathcart's Hill Major General Sir John Campbell commands the (4th) Division, and having received a message from him offering assistance if I would come there, I presented myself to him and at once told him my difficulties about a servant and was immediately invited to take up my quarters with him. [13th April.]

Up at H.Q. Sparling and William slept in Fenton's tent, which was full of photographic apparatus and material. Fenton himself preferred to rely on hospitality for his sleeping quarters and eating arrangements.

"Meanwhile", said Sir John, "come down and take a glass of sherry", and he led the way into a hole in the ground, a natural cavern which he had found and took possession of just before the storm of the 14th of November. [It was on Cathcart's Hill, near the flagstaff.]

I tried to take a picture of the town but the day, though fine, was hazy, and I could not succeed. I took some nice groups, however, and some portraits, one of the general sitting at the door of his tent (*Pl. 50*). At seven we sat down to dinner in the cavern, the general, his aide Captain Hume, and Captain Layard, a brother of the traveller, and a very comfortable party and jolly picture we made, a huge barrel of beer in one corner and the arms stuck into nooks in the rocks giving us the look of a party of smugglers. There was a novelty at dinner—a salad of dandelion leaves: very good it was with oil and vinegar. Sir John gave me his marquee to sleep in, and I could not have picked out a cleaner residence. It is about 200 yards nearer Sebastopol [about 1½ miles distant] than any other tent, and on the slope towards it, so that as I lay in bed with the door open I could see the fire.

VISIT TO THE BATTERY

I forgot to say that as soon as my work was done I resolved to go down and have a look from the hill which I had visited a day or two before. I got ensconced behind a big stone, laid my glass on the top, and began to look for the damage done to the Russian batteries by our fire. I had a good survey and found that the banks of earth of which they were constructed were much shattered in some places, but from the fire kept up by them there was no appearance of their guns being dismounted. I had forgotten all about my former alarms when, still intent upon my observations, I was startled by a long whir just over my head. Before I had ducked the ball was bounding up the hill behind, kicking up earth and stones. I found the only damage I got was a scratch on the forehead in my eagerness to humble myself. Feeling a strong desire to go and see what they were doing in the battery in front of me, I walked down the slope of the hill and had the satisfaction of seeing several balls and shells go by, most of them striking a little to the left.

In the battery I was very comfortable, for the wall sheltered me, only it struck me as a queer sensation to hear the balls thumping into the earth against which one was leaning. Others came topping the ramparts and whistling overhead. I have a pass for the trenches, so was not turned out or put under arrest. In chatting with the officer in command I was rather amused (being conscious of my own trepidation of spirits) to hear him say that he had watched me coming down the hill to see if I would hurry my pace when the balls passed, and that I had not shown any signs of noticing them. I did not undeceive him.

There was a sailor lying wounded in the battery [probably the Diamond Battery, so called because it was manned by sailors from H.M.S. "Diamond"] and during a lull in the fire they put him on a stretcher and two sailors carried him up the hill. They got halfway up when the fire began again; it was very droll to see them struggle to one side whenever the whistle of a shot came near. The officer in command offered to bet that if a shell dropped near them they would drop their burden and run, and that the wounded man would get on his legs and follow. They got him up safely. When I thought it time to go back a young officer volunteered to show me a place on the hill where I might sit in safety and watch. We set off at full speed up the hill and were not long in getting to the indicated spot. I find it is much worse to walk away from fire than fronting it; I felt a strong inclination to look over my shoulder to see if anything was coming.

Next night I dined with General Barnard, but this will do for this letter as it is a fine day and I am going to take a field day on General Pennefather's division (*Pl. 72*). [Lieut.-General (Sir) John Lysaght Pennefather commanded the 2nd Division at Inkerman.]

THE VALLEY OF THE SHADOW OF DEATH

Apl. 24th 1855.

The last week I have been up at the front, have taken a complete panorama of the camp and town, living all the time at Sir John Campbell's, who has treated me just as if I were one of his staff. Yesterday after finishing the last picture of the panorama I got Sir John to lend me a couple of mules and took my carriage down a ravine known by the name of the Valley of the Shadow of Death [*not* the scene of the charge of the Light Brigade] from the quantity of Russian balls that have fallen in it. I had been down to the caves where our men lie in the daytime when on duty in the trenches two days before to choose the best view; if you remember, I went with Wilkinson and our progress was stopped by a ball [see page 57]. Since the siege re-opened it is very dangerous to go down there, as all the balls from the Redan, the Barrack battery, and the Garden battery are fired at the Chapman's battery, and those that go too high come over into this valley. Though the fire still continues and is at times (especially from eight to ten in the morning and from three to four p.m.) very warm, there have been latterly lulls in which the ear is left in peace, and when I was in the valley on Saturday not a shot came over.

We were detained in setting off and so got down unluckily just about 3 p.m. yesterday. I took the van down nearly as far as I intended it to go and then went forward to find out the chosen spot. I had scarcely started when a dash of dust behind the battery before us showed that something was on the way to us. We could not see it but another flood of earth nearer showed that it was coming straight, and in a moment we saw it bounding up towards us. It turned off when near, and where it went I did not see, as a shell came over about the same spot, knocked its fuse out and joined the mass of its brethren without bursting. It was plain that the line of fire was upon the very spot I had chosen, so very reluctantly I put up with another view of the valley 100 yards short of the best point. I brought the van down and fixed the camera, and while levelling it another ball came in a more slanting direction, touching the rear of the battery as the others, but instead of coming up the road, bounded on to the hill on our left about 50 yards from us and came down right to us, stopping at our feet. I picked it up and put it into the van; I hope to make you a present of it. After this no more came near, though plenty passed on each side. We were there an hour and a half and got two good pictures (*Pl. 51*), returning in triumph with our trophies, finishing the day's work by taking the van to the mortar battery (*Pl. 52*) on the top of the hill in front of the Light Division. The Russians seem as if it were their plan just to fire enough to make us exhaust our ammunition. It is evident they have no fear of our taking the south side, and they are now as busy as bees constructing new batteries on the north side.

In the middle of last week everyone was at Cathcart's Hill looking out for the explosion of a great mine which the French had driven under the Garden fort; the time was announced for 4 p.m. As I had private information of the fact I was ready with my camera at the precise time, but no event coming off I shut up, and it was soon announced that it was postponed till half past six. Long after that time the hill was crowded with officers and soldiers. We had an active discussion going on as to whether the mine had exploded or not, general opinion saying "Yes". Anyhow, there was a very sharp musketry fire soon after, lasting for about an hour, and we heard next morning that the French had taken the battery and then retreated from it, not thinking the position tenable.

A night or two afterwards [19th April] the English attacked and took one of the rifle pits which the French had tried to take on the 22nd March when they got such a complete licking. Our men took and held it and worked so hard in connecting it with our trenches during the night that next morning the Russians were forced to abandon the rest. I was at Balaclava that night (19th April) and coming up early in the morning found every officer I knew looking very grave, for the Colonel of the 77th Regiment, Egerton, who was much liked, had been killed, and a Captain Lemprière, also a young and very able officer of whom Egerton was very fond. Hallewell tells me that Lemprière was shot dead in the attack, that Egerton took him up and said "I'll carry my poor boy into the trenches", then came back and was shot through the mouth and brain. They were buried side by side next day. [The rifle pit was henceforth known as "Egerton's pit".] All the army seem to long to take the field and have done with this constant frittering away of valuable lives. When they do go out to attack the Russians it will be a very different affair from Alma [when the allies did not follow up their victory by pursuing the Russians]. The Russians have got accustomed to licking the French and don't care for them.

There was a very pretty scene here some days since. Omar Pasha turned out the troops for a reconnaissance towards the Tchernaya, accompanied by French cavalry. We did not know of it, but saw puffs of smoke rising from the passes of the hills beyond Balaclava, which at first we thought must be wreaths of mist, as it was morning. I called up Sir John and with our glasses we made out three lines near the crest of a hill far off, the top lines firing volleys of musketry at something on the further slope. I saw them coming back at night. Every day has brought something to interest or excite, and there is so much worth telling that I can only just mention what occurs to me, and generally it is the latest impression which you get in my letters and which for the moment effaces its predecessors.

There are two things I have enjoyed whilst staying with Sir John: the first, lying in bed with the tent door open listening and watching the incessant fire of shot, shell and musketry; again about seven there is often a pause and then while breakfast is getting ready I pick out a nice stone to lean against and lie down and listen to the larks overhead and watch the dreamy-looking town, which is at that time generally half bathed in mist; an occasional white puff shows that they are watchful in the quiet place, and sometimes two opposing batteries have a little chat all alone, and I establish myself as self-appointed arbiter of the event, giving equal praise to the Malakoff when it drops a shell neatly in the rear of the batteries, as to Gordon's battery when it makes the dust fly in an embrasure of the Malakoff. The town *may*, I believe, be taken bit by bit as they are trying to do, but it will take an awful time and cost a terrible waste of life. Everyone almost here has made up his mind there will be peace, and seems to be getting homesick. This would disappear at once if there were any chance of taking the field.

April 29th 1855.

After leaving the valley where the shots are so thick, I took the van round to the head of the next ravine and up to the rear of the mortar battery, and as this spot is forbidden to everyone but staff officers and people on duty, I had a little quiet for a few hours each day, having hard work, however, in carrying my collodion plates backwards and forwards from the van to the camera. The views here were not very good, as nobody being in front I could make no foreground, and the town is so far off that in itself it is no picture. All the sketches seen at home seem to err in making it much too near and in making the details too large in order to obtain distinctness.

There has been little firing going on the last week. An occasional shot from advanced batteries and several shells well aimed from a mortar battery and from a ship in the sound have formed the principal part of the day's amusement. At night the firing has generally been brisk, but with little result except with great waste of French powder. Every morning sees some fresh work commenced or finished by the Russians, sometimes a new rifle pit is made in the night, sometimes two or more are connected together by a trench so as to form a kind of advanced battery, some-times one detects the beginning of new works on the other side of the harbour. The hills beyond are getting dotted over with white tents and the sides of the hills roughened with the burrows in which they live. Their principal burying ground, too, is getting rapidly peopled. They do not bury as we do in single graves, but make large pits which they fill with bodies and then heap over with earth.

Our sick are, I believe, on the increase. There have been several cases of cholera last week, principally in the Light Division, which seems to be placed in rather an unfavourable position.

The English forces have been animated by the arrival of Lady George Paget, Lady Stratford and the two daughters. I met them yesterday riding with a very large escort of Light Dragoon officers and staff swells along the heights overlooking the plains where the cavalry charge took place. There have also arrived several new regiments and lots of horses for the Artillery and Cavalry. All seem to be expecting the order to advance into the interior, the expectation of peace having grown small: as for taking the town on the present system, it is a perfect farce. The Mamelon, the most advanced of the Russian earthworks, is as neat in its external finish as if a ball or shell had never touched it. The French make much fuss and seem to attack every night, but one generally finds each morning that the Russians have made some slight advance towards them, instead of being gradually driven into the town. Our men keep what they take and waste no powder, but they cannot advance until the French have delivered them from the danger of being taken in the flank.

Were it not for the great longing I have now to be off, and the too great fatigue which I go through in consequence, my time passes pleasantly. I have dined at Sir

Richard England's and enjoyed my visit. Dined the next day with General Penne-father and his staff, and the day after with Colonel Benton and Wilkinson at Halle-well's. I found with him Colonel Airey [Assistant Quartermaster-General], the brother of General Airey; we got on uncommonly well.

Today is Sunday [29th April]. It is wet, cold and dismal. I lay trying to get an extra snooze but could not, after repeated trials, find out which was the softest part of the boards, so began to read.

After breakfast I walked over to General Bosquet's [Commander of the 2nd French Corps]. The General received me very kindly and invited me to mess with himself and staff when I go to his camp, which I intend to do in a couple of days. He is a fine looking man with a broad face full of good temper.

Afterwards I rode down to Balaclava; there was no church parade on account of the rain. Instead of finding William there, he had gone up to the camp to amuse himself, thinking, I suppose, that as it was Sunday he was at liberty to leave his post. Hallewell was in town too, and called for me to ride back with him, but I had fallen asleep quite worn out with hard work, and when roused felt very loathe to ride eight miles through the mud and rain, so turned in till tea time, since when I have written this note, which by its rambling incoherence must bear the marks of being written by a man only half awake.

I am sorry to say the "Hecla" leaves this week. She has been quite a home to me and I shall be very sorry to say goodbye to her and her captain. He has promised me to call at No. 2. [No. 2 Albert Terrace, Primrose Hill, Fenton's home.]

Two days since, Ismael Pasha, commander of the Egyptian troops, came to me. I made some good groups of him and his suite (*Pl. 69*). There was a Nubian slave and a Copt pipe-bearer. I am getting surfeited with good pictures now, and want sadly to go back. Tell Annie there are two Russian boys here (*Pl. 63*) who would both like to come to England. Alma and Inkerman, such are their names: one is an orphan, the other has or had his parents in the town. They went out nutting last autumn and were taken. They cried sadly, but now would cry to go back.

VISIT TO THE VALLEY OF INKERMAN

May 5th 1855.

Yesterday was May day, and a lovely day we had. I got Sir George Brown to sit to me; he was very amiable, put on his uniform and a cocked hat and did just as I wished him (*Pl. 70*). He asked me to dine with him at seven.

In the afternoon I rode with Hallewell to Inkerman, got halfway down the slope, took the bridles off our horses, let them graze, and we lay basking in the sun and looking through the glass at a piquet of Cossacks along the Tchernaya and a regiment of infantry being drilled about two miles off, in front of the lines which the Russians have made across the country where the Mackenzie farm road comes down.

Wherever the ground is not quite safe to go on (where it is commanded by Russian batteries) it is quite surprising to see the mass of wild flowers with which the ground is covered; all over the steep sides of the Inkerman the grass and flowers are gradually budding; the pieces of torn cloth, ragged caps, shoes without soles, now form the principal indications of the struggle which took place there. I have been there now three times, and with people who were in the battle, and none of them can tell me where any of the principal incidents took place. Everybody was busy about what immediately concerned their own corps or department, and saw nothing of the general action. I was told a new version of the French attack on the Russian flank. It was said that a French regiment mounted the hill to meet the Russians, was observed at once when on the top to turn right about face and come down again. An A.D.C. rode up to the Colonel and said, "Mais monsieur, are you retreating?". The answer was, "Voilà les Russes."!

On our return just before dinner Sir George Brown sent for Hallewell and told him something that made him come home dancing and kicking and emptying a tumbler of champagne, when he grew able to inform us that an expedition was to start off the next day [3rd May] by sea somewhere or other, and that he had been chosen to go with it as Deputy Adjutant-General. At dinner Sir George was very silent about the matter, merely telling us that he was to have 4,000 English and 800 Turks under his orders and that he meant to take some of his own staff with him. That night and this morning there has been such a scene of packing and rejoicing among those chosen for the expedition, and sulking and trying to look as if they did not care among those going to stay here, that you would have thought they were all schoolboys. No one knows where they are going: some say Eupatoria to join the grand attack on the Russian rear, others Kertch, and some Odessa. Hallewell is off and is now on board ship, leaving me heir to his tent and servant. [This was the first Kertch expedition, called off a few days later. See page 74.]

Last night there was some small firing between the French and Russians and it was said the former took a trench from the Russians and actually kept it!

Have you seen that picture in the 'Illustrated London News' of Sebastopol from the sea? It has caused a great deal of astonishment and amusement here, as it is a regular "Punch" sketch.

AT GENERAL BOSQUET'S QUARTERS

May 6th. The day before yesterday I moved my van to General Bosquet's quarters. I did not stop there that night as I had engaged to dine with Sir John Campbell and to sleep at his quarters. After breakfast yesterday I went thence to General Bosquet's. I soon got all the staff round me waiting a trial of my skill. I made a group with General Cissé the Chief of the Staff in the centre (*Pl. 58*). We were soon called to breakfast and though I had done very well at Sir John's at 8½ I was ready again for a French spread at 10½. General Bosquet made me sit close to him and was very kind, I like him much. After breakfast the officers got together a quantity of soldiers of different corps, Zouaves, chasseurs, &c. I made several fine pictures of them (*Pl. 53*). In the afternoon a cantinière was brought up. I made first a picture of her by herself and then a group in which she is giving relief to a wounded soldier (*Pl. 54*). I took a view or two with my newly arrived Ross lenses, with which I am delighted. When I got back I found a tent pitched for me. Sparling had brought up my bed and mat for wrapper (the blankets are stolen). I had the mattress on the ground and the wrapper over it, got some thread and patched up my old coat which is nearly in tatters, and by the time this was done was called to dinner.

The dinner was not bad, but less comfortable than at our English officers' quarters, but I enjoyed it immensely for the General was very chatty. He talked about England and France, asked a good deal about Russia [Fenton refers to his journey in 1852 to Kiev, St. Petersburg and Moscow], and then began to talk about the war and the mismanagement of it and the causes of the want of success hitherto. It was very interesting. When he rose we all got up and I was about to take my leave, when he made me go with him out into the starlight and began to tell me about his first interview with Napoleon, when the expedition was first thought of. Then he got to the battles of Alma and Inkerman, describing them and pointing out what in his opinion ought to have been done, and what result might have been obtained after each of these battles if the army had been under one head. He talked much of the horror which he felt at all the terrible scenes of suffering and death which he had witnessed here, and said it was not possible for anyone to have a greater dislike of war than a soldier like him, whose life for the last twenty years had been spent in burying his friends. He then got upon politics, English and French, upon which I enlarged in a way that would have made your hair stand on end, for I have grown more Radical since I got here. I could not help now and then thinking what a queer *tableau vivant* I was forming part of, *tête à tête* under the stars with one of the most celebrated men of the day, discussing the conduct and capacity of the great guns of our acquaintance with much more freedom than if I formed part of a special commission. I see and hear many things here which I should never have known, had I been placed in any official position. Fortunately I know how to forget things which it would be mischievous to repeat.

General Bosquet is very good to take (*Pl. 55*), resembling much the portrait of

Napoleon when he began to grow stout, only there is an expression of frankness and good temper which does not exist in Napoleon's portrait. He has promised me horses to convey my van, and all that I need while staying with him. His staff are very nice fellows.

To William Agnew.

May 18th and 20th.

I send you herewith a few portraits which are worth engraving and will serve to keep up the attention of the public until my return. I make very slow progress, though as far as lies in my power no time is lost. I am very anxious to return home, as my interests are suffering in my absence, but I cannot make up my mind to leave until I have secured pictures of the persons and subjects likely to be historically interesting.

I am at present living with General Bosquet, who treats me as one of his own family. Unfortunately the tents in which he placed me are in a damp low place and when the late storm of rain came on, sleeping on the ground, I was attacked with dysentry and obliged to leave and go down to Kadikoi for quiet and medical aid. I am now perfectly cured. They have given me a tent in a better situation, and yesterday and today I have been at work at Inkerman, where my wagon is placed so that it can be seen by only one of the Russian batteries. We have had several shells and cannon balls close past us today, only one of which was, so far as I could tell, aimed at us, and that did not come within twenty yards. It is not amusing at all to hear the whir of cannon balls approaching.

I was today in front of one of the French batteries when they were relieving guard. The Russians can see the relief coming and always fire across the valley at these times. I saw the flash of a battery in front and stood still to wait for the shot. I heard it coming through the air right towards us and waited in some anxiety to know how near it would be. As it approached, it was with great satisfaction that I heard it pass over my head instead of making a nearer acquaintance with my person.

In the afternoon I made a slight sketch in colour of the valley of Inkerman and had nearly finished it when some riflemen down below saw me, and their fourth shot came so near that I thought it best to decamp. Generally they are very civil and the greater part of the day leave me alone. Tomorrow morning I move the van to the rear of the battery where the Guards sustained such severe losses. I have got splendid stereoscopic views of the ruins of Inkerman and the valley.

These were not the usual small binocular pictures taken for Sir David Brewster's lenticular stereoscope, but fairly large views taken with two identical cameras standing side by side, for Sir Charles Wheatstone's reflecting stereoscope.

There is far more here than I could do in six months! I am sorry that I am obliged to return so soon, but I shall bring back, after all, a very good selection of subjects.

AT GENERAL BARNARD'S

(continued) *Sunday*, May 20th/55. I have left Bosquet's and am now with General Barnard for a couple of days. It is so hot now that nothing can be done after nine in the morning. The officers of the 10th, who have just come from India, complain very much and say that the sun burns much more here. General Canrobert has given up the command of the army to Pélissier and resumes the command of a division. This is at his own request, as he says that he feels himself unequal to the task of directing so large an army. Pélissier is a good head fellow, not very intellectual but energetic and unscrupulous. He will not be long without setting the army in movement, and he won't care about a few thousand lives if he has an object to gain.

I rode over this morning to the seaside seven miles off with General Barnard's son at six in the morning to bathe; it was very delightful. I shall come back now as soon as I have got Lord Raglan's portrait as my time is being wasted. I can see no sketches worth buying here [for publication by Agnew]. Major Hallewell sent his panorama to the Queen; if you can obtain that it will be worth having. Simpson only makes pencil sketches on the spot and colours them at home. The only French artist [Constantin Guys] I have seen does the same.

I am sitting in one of General Barnard's marquees; they are double tents and much cooler than the others. It is open to the air on every side and there is a nice breeze, but the perspiration is pouring down my face as if I had been riding for a cup. I am afraid when the army moves they will suffer dreadfully from the heat and from thirst.

THE KERTCH EXPEDITION

The expedition on which Fenton's friend Major Hallewell departed on May 3rd was a joint expedition to the Kertch peninsular, of some 12,000 men under the supreme command of Sir George Brown. The object was to destroy the forts guarding the entrance to the Sea of Azov and then to ravage the coastal supply ports and shipping there. On telegraphic orders sent personally by Napoleon III, General Canrobert, the French Commander-in-Chief, was forced to recall the

French fleet sailing towards Kertch, for the Emperor wanted the vessels to fetch reserve troops from Constantinople for all-out field operations to be led by himself. The whole expedition was abandoned, to the wrath of everyone; Canrobert resigned the chief command and resumed that of the 1st Division.

His successor, the resolute General Pélissier (later created Duc de Malakoff), did not give way to the Emperor's whims and the expedition started afresh on the evening of 22nd May and morning of the 23rd.

At noon on the 24th a squadron of eight English and four French steamers and six gunboats, carrying a land force of some 16,000 British, French and Turkish troops under the command of Sir George Brown, disembarked at Ambalaki, a few miles south of Kertch. The Russians shortly afterwards blew up their batteries, starting with that on nearby Cape St. Paul, and abandoned their positions: their commander, Baron Wrangel, having to defend the road linking his forces with the main army, which was also the supply road to Sebastopol, was prepared to abandon the seven coastal batteries. The Russians having withdrawn from Kertch and Yenikale which commanded the straits into the Sea of Azov, the allied army marched through Kertch and occupied Yenikale. Here, and in Kertch, disgraceful scenes of pillaging took place, which were not entirely confined to the Turks and the French.

Roger Fenton accompanied the expedition, which he regarded rather in the nature of a holiday trip, without his photographic apparatus, which, indeed, would probably have been smashed sooner or later.

> May 26th. Yenikale,
> Sea of Azov.

Just look at the address of this letter and then at your map to find out exactly where Yenikale is, and then set yourself into some easy chair and read the story that I am going to write you about the life of the last few days led by the British, French and Turkish forces under the command of Sir G. Brown, and especially about the adventures of that important portion of it represented by the writer of this letter.

I think in my last I told you that I had left General Bosquet's and was at General Barnard's hill. I stayed there two days, and then moved to Sir. R. England's at five in the morning of the 22nd, intending to remain a day there and then go on to Headquarters. I worked till breakfast time, and then heard that the expedition to Kertch was about to be renewed. Having been ill again with diarrhoea, though not so badly as at first, I decided that it would do me good to have a little change, so galloped off to Headquarters, got an order from Lord Raglan to go as an engineer officer on Colonel Gordon's staff, no civilian being allowed to accompany the expedition.

I took my fur wrapper, carpet bag and the case of my bed to lay on the ground at night, and set off to Balaclava. Got on board the "Bahiana", a steamer on which officers of the staff were to embark, and then set myself to watch what was going on. Immense excitement and confusion: people getting into the wrong ship and being knocked out, horses being hoisted on board and stowed in the hold; and on deck, officers' servants arranging their masters' luggage, Commissariat mule-drivers, soldiers and sailors tumbling over one another. We had a jolly dinner at four, hock, port, sherry and champagne, all the while this was going on. Hallewell, Colonel Airey and a Colonel More of my acquaintance were of the party.

Next morning [23rd] we got out of the harbour, waited outside for a ship we were to tow, and then set off with it along the south coast of the Crimea. We passed first along a succession of precipitous rocks without any houses or pathways till about noon, when we came to a slope on which were a number of farm houses and villas, and a little later we passed Prince Woronzoff's mansion near Yalta [head-quarters of the British delegation during the Yalta Conference in February 1945]. We did not see it well, for the heat fog came on at sunrise.

The following morning we were off Cape Takli with a great number of trans-ports, steamers, gun boats, two French men-of-war and three English, one of which was the "Royal Albert". It was a beautiful sight. The sea had been as smooth as a pond all the way, the sky without a cloud, and as the fleet went round the Cape and steered on towards the Straits it formed a beautiful perspective. We went down slowly, the steam gunboats leading the way towards the entrance of the Straits [of Kertch].

As we got near the land we could see a great lot of vessels making off up the Straits, and then two of our steamers and one of the French went off after them apparently, but when the first, which was an English vessel, came opposite to the point, a battery opened fire upon her and she returned the fire. By this time the fleet was near the land and boats were laid out with troops in, ready for landing. We were all looking out with our telescopes to see what resistance would be put up to the landing and great excitement arose when a cloud of dust was seen on the brow of a hill in front and a body of cavalry was seen galloping down towards the landing place. As they were coming near, one of the gunboats fired a shell right into the middle of them, on which they scattered into small groups and kept riding about watching, not attempting resistance. As the boats with the troops approached the beach there suddenly shot up from the fort on the point [the battery on Cape St. Paul] a great column of smoke with a loud explosion. The Russians had blown it up, and very soon there followed several other explosions, one of which caused a tremendous concussion. We saw the garrison going away up the hillside, and there went up a great cheer through the fleet, for it was evident that the Russians were not strong enough to resist the landing.

THE LANDING AT AMBALAKI

The French landed first in beautiful style, then our men, marching away as they landed to get on to the ridge of the high land above the flat beach. This beach seemed only a narrow strip from the ship but it was above a mile wide.

Hallewell and Airey went off as soon as the first lot of troops landed, to superintend the disembarkation of the rest of the horses and transport corps. I stopped on board till dinner time, 4 p.m., thinking it wise to stow as much good victuals as I could before starting. Every man had been ordered to take two days' provisions. Hallewell's servant drew mine, but I took a fair supply internally and then accompanied the captain of our ship in his own boat ashore. What a sight! In the morning, a beautiful beach covered with long rough grass and wild flowers, two or three fishing boats with their nets, a couple of stone cottages with thatched roofs, and a low sandy plain stretching to a ridge of high ground behind, had formed the whole of the picture. Now, the beach was strewn with baggage of every description, horses were splashing through the water to the shore, men dressed in every kind of garment that was ever worn, were walking about, scrambling, swearing, shouting and laughing—a vast deal of the latter. Servants were keeping guard over their masters' baggage horses. My bag and bed were thrown on the shore; I sat down on them and began to calculate my chances of getting any further. I had brought no horse, being told that we should go right to Kertch and that a horse would only be in the way, but I saw that all my advisers had brought both horses and servants. The medical profession came to my aid. Dr. Alexander, Deputy Interpreter-General, had four horses, and told his servant to hoist my baggage on to a pack saddle with his, offering me at the same time a corner of his tent till we could get somewhere. You may be sure I did not refuse.

After wandering about enjoying the odd scenes that met me on every side, and being scandalized by the burning of some cottages by the French and the wrecking of another, the question was raised, Where are we to encamp for the night? The Dr. objected to the present site as feverish-looking in spite of its agreeable aspect, and enquiring for Sir G. Brown's headquarters we were directed by Hallewell to some houses on the ridge about a mile off. As it was getting dusk there was no time to lose, so the baggage was hurried on to the horses' backs and we set off, the Dr. and I riding. The ascent was so steep that the loads of two of the pack horses broke down. Lots of others, French and English, were in the same plight, everybody entreating his neighbour's assistance and abusing his own horses and mules, who resented the insults by kicking at the baggage as it lay about.

We got up at last, and I unpacked and prepared for bivouacking. The house we were directed to was close by and we congratulated ourselves on being in a good situation for an early start next morning. I had picked up a lot of barrel-staves to make a fire with. Before pitching the tents, we enquired if the General were at the house indicated, and were told that the English were away along the ridge to the right. Everybody telling the same story, we had nothing to do but to load the horses again and set off. This was done for better or worse, but generally worse, for every hundred yards something or other dropped off and the whole load turned round (it was nothing like as jolly as our landing on the beach had been, all sunshine and fun). We went along very slowly through long tangled grass and thistles, guided by the light of a large hayrick burning fiercely, showing, as figures passed between us and the flames, that others were going in the same direction. There was a light a long way off towards which we steered, making very slow progress from the constant breakdowns of our baggage. We met people now and then who told us to go towards the light and we should find the English quarters. As we got near, the light became a series of watch fires, and the sounds rising from them told me that they were French. We were then directed on to another light far off in the same line, which as we approached turned out to be another French regiment. It was midnight, we were too tired to speak to one another. As it was evident that we had lost our way, the Dr. and I took council and resolved to camp where we were.

At half past three, before the sun was fairly up, we were roused by the noise of the French getting ready to march. We got up, with a very ill grace though, and the men struck the tents lest we should have to go at once. The wood I had carried was soon split up and the kettle on with the tea in it, half a chicken was produced, and as the sun got up and we got fed, we recovered our jollity—all but the horses, for we had no water for them, having only got by a long walk by one of the men enough water to make tea. Meanwhile one of the staff came up and told us that we had been quite right at first and that Sir G. Brown and they *did* sleep in the very house at which we had at first stopped!

Not a soul of the inhabitants were to be seen; all had left, we saw some of the last with our glasses in the morning from the ships, going away in carts, and one group left the village while the French were firing shells into it to protect the disembarkation. While we were packing up (more carefully this time) the French had marched up in the van followed by the Turks, and the 79th, 42nd, 93rd and 71st Highland regiments brought up the rear. They had all disappeared behind some low hills before we started; however, we soon overtook our men, and a beautiful sight it was to see them marching down the reverse of the hills on which we stood. There were no Russian troops in sight.

ARRIVAL AT KERTCH

In about four miles we came to Kertch, a very pretty town beautifully situated along the bay. All the authorities were gone and the best houses had their shutters closed, but groups of Tartars were standing by the side of the streets, taking off their hats and smiling most obsequiously. A good many of the Russian smaller shop keepers were still there, and many Greeks. They all looked very frightened, and with good reason so far as the French and Turks were concerned. A good many women stood in the doors and peeped out of the windows. By Sir G. Brown's orders no one was allowed to break the ranks; sentries were placed at the doors of the principal houses and public buildings and the army marched through the town without stopping except for a few minutes when something ahead obstructed the march. It was evident that it was not intended to go on to the Sea of Azov, where in the night we had seen heavy firing in the distance, returned by some of our steamers. We expect to return to Balaclava within a week, but the mail is just leaving so I must defer the rest. I am writing this in a house [in Yenikale], the windows mostly smashed, Turks and French putting in their heads to look for plunder and breaking the rest of the windows when they see there is nothing for them. When one of the Turks sent a whole window frame in shivers into the room, I kicked out and hammered his stupid head, and handed him over to the English.

May 28th.

I hope you will have received my last letter for this is only a continuation. I think at the end of it Sir G. Brown and I were marching into Kertch. We passed round a bit of marshy water, then came to some large enclosed buildings, one of which I was informed by Colonel Gordon was a manufactory of shot and would be destroyed immediately. We entered the town between two handsome buildings of Greek architecture, and whitewashed like all Russian buildings. There was a halt in the town during which some of our officers managed to get acquainted with some of the inhabitants who could speak French, and they managed to make themselves much at home, though in a respectable manner. None of the men were allowed to break the ranks and they got nothing but a little water which the people brought out to them; it was amusing to watch the struggle when a bucket of water was brought out, it was emptied in no time.

Kertch is a beautiful place, the town modern and very regularly built, the situation is very beautiful, reminding one of the pictures of Naples. In the rear a projecting shoulder of one of the hills behind almost cuts the place in two, and halfway up is a museum built like a Greek temple, while above is a tomb called the tomb of Mithridates, which appears most suspiciously of modern construction.

The town, the architecture of which was mostly in the Greek style, was built round Mount Mithridates, on the summit of which stood a small modern Ionic "temple", the grave of a Governor of Kertch, which Fenton—in common with W. H. Russell—erroneously supposed to be the tomb of Mithridates. Lower down the hill was the Museum in Doric style, with a valuable collection of ancient sculpture and vases, which was sacked by the troops.

After half an hour's halt we marched on along a good road by the sea till we came to a mass of buildings on the point of land which terminates Kertch bay, and which was used by the Russians as a quarantine station. It was quite deserted, some of the buildings were blown up, others showed marks of the shot of our gunboats. I hoped that we were going to stop here, for the heat was oppressive and the men were parched with thirst and choked with dust, but after a short halt we marched along the high ground from which could be seen the whole of the army in advance. The country itself is beautiful, a vast extent of grassy slopes covered with long coarse herbage, which in itself was a delightful prospect to eyes accustomed too long to the bare barren red earth of the camp before Sebastopol. The descent to the sea was bordered with fine houses and villas in the midst of young plantations.

PLUNDERING

Our army was marching in columns in beautiful order, scarcely a man falling out from the ranks. On each side and in front as far as we could see, the country was covered with stragglers, Turkish and French, but principally the latter, intent on plunder. We could see the French rushing through the plantations into the houses and coming out again laden with fowls, geese, looking-glasses, chairs, ladies' dresses and everything useful or useless that they could lay their hands on. As they got to the contents of wine casks they got more outrageous, discharging their muskets right and left at fowls, pigs and birds. Shots came whistling amongst us, and, of course, remonstrances with half-drunken men were useless; their own officers never attempted to interfere. On the left a lot of French soldiers were driving along a herd of milch cows and mares which they had captured. I could hear them speculating as to whether those cursed English were to share with them in the spoil. If any Russian troops had come down upon us, they would have punished the French pretty severely, for the lust for plunder had destroyed all appearance of discipline among them.

Some delay occurred here and while we were all lying on the grass, boiling in the intense heat, there came up a poor woman with her old mother wringing her hands and complaining that the soldiers were carrying off her only cow. The General was near and he at once ordered Hallewell to go with the poor people and try to recover their worldly goods for them. In a short time she came back driving the cow, but meantime as the herd was obliged to stop we set to work to milk the cows. While I held Dr. Alexander's horse and procured a cup, he milked the cows, and each time the cup was half filled brought and filled it up with water and we shared it. This was repeated several times to the great disgust of the French soldiers in charge, who swore awfully but not hard enough to stop us. In the last cup we mixed a little brandy on condition of sharing the tipple with the owner of the brandy. This seasonable supply set me up again as I had no provisions, Hallewell's servant, who was some miles in the rear, still having mine in his care.

Just as the milk was done the poor woman came up, but when she tried to pass through the line of French soldiers they refused to let the cow pass, threatening the woman with their bayonets. We got savage at this and turned on them, and being very much in earnest made them see that it was safer not to molest the poor creatures. The younger of the women, terrified and overcome with fatigue and excitement, went into hysterics and fainted, and when the Dr. had brought her round I could not help laughing, in spite of my anger, at seeing them rush at their deliverers and attempt to kiss our feet. The embarrassment of the kisses was very droll. To ensure their not being plundered after we left, Dr. Alexander wrote out a pass for them in French and English and signed it with a magnificent flourish of "Interpreter General" after his name.

As we got on, the disorder became greater, the stragglers were more drunk, the cries and shouts more savage, the firing of muskets and the whizzing of shot past our ears more continual, and it was evident that all control over the French army was gone and that we should have a terrible night.

The army halted on some heights on the other side of which was said to be the town of Yenikale, though nothing was to be seen of it from where we were except some Tartar cottages, whose inhabitants had to look on quietly while the soldiers —French, Turks and English—went in and helped themselves to everything they wanted. There were four windmills just behind these cottages, built of wood; in ten minutes these were in ruins and nothing left but the stone bases on which they were built.

As the troops were taking up their quarters, I began to think about looking for mine. It was then 4 p.m. and I had had nothing to eat since five in the morning. I was quite faint and would have given anything for the bite of an old crust. Hallewell was off with the General, Colonel Gordon to whom I was attached was nowhere to be found, Dr. Alexander on whom I relied for supplies and whom I had kept in sight during the day, helping him when called to the assistance of anyone threatened with sunstroke, of which several cases occurred during the day, was nowhere to be found or heard of.

OCCUPATION OF YENIKALE

I resolved to enter the town and look for General Brown's headquarters as the surest way of finding my own. Accompanying a picket of Highlanders, I went over the hill and down towards the sea, entering the gateway of the fort, the pathway of which was choked with stones and fragments of timber caused by the explosion of a magazine which the Russians had set fire to before leaving. Scrambling over this, we got on to a platform of level ground, on the right of which was a bank covered with the ruins of a great explosion. Seeing a large building before us, we went to it and found a hospital with the beds laid down comfortably side by side on a raised platform like a double desk measuring the whole length of the building. The ground was strewn with fragments of wood and stone, and the windows were all broken by the explosion. The pewter pots for the drink of the patients were ranged in order on a shelf. I took one and at the end of the terrace found a well of beautiful water and had a good pull at it without troubling myself whether it was poisoned or not. There was a French picket and a couple of officers in the fort, but with that exception all was perfectly solitary.

Close by was another long building: an officer told me that it was another hospital and that he found there four Russian soldiers wounded and unable to move, without food or drink. They held up their hands and made signs for help, but it was night before in the confusion anyone could be appointed to attend upon them.

Going to the side next the sea I saw a new battery of nine heavy guns, 36-pounders, beautifully made, and pointing in the direction of our ships. They were spiked, of course. The platform on which they were placed was scarcely finished and it was evident that the Russians had been surprised in the midst of preparations caused by the countermanded expedition three weeks back. In front was a floating battery. Altogether there were thirty-two guns captured in the place, most of them quite new and of beautiful construction.

DISGRACEFUL SCENES OF PILLAGING

Going out of the fort I came to the town itself, which lies under the cliff and up its sides. There was a terrible scene: French, Turks, and I am sorry to say a few Highlanders, were breaking into the houses, smashing the windows, dragging out everything portable and breaking what they could not carry away. The inhabitants had all fled with the exception of the Tartars and a few Russians, amongst whom was the priest; from the treatment of those that were left, it was lucky that they had.

Disgusted with the sight and unable to help it except by pitching into our own men, I hunted for the General's quarters but could not find them. I now went back to the camp in search of Dr. Alexander but could not find him either. He had been sent for to look at two of our men who had been shot by the stray French bullets; one of them was shot dead, and the other was badly wounded in the head. I heard that he had got a room in the town, so after begging a bit of biscuit from some officers of the 42nd and receiving an invite to take my chance with them if I could not find my own supplies, I went down again and found Dr. A.'s quarters but not himself. They were at a house on the beach, only one storey high, as are most of the houses here. French and Turks were passing by, thrusting their heads through the windows and trying to get into the courtyard, which was defended by the Dr.'s three servants. I saw that the Dr. would have quite enough to do to take care of himself, so got my fur blanket and set off with it up the hill again. On the way I met Hallewell, who had lost his servant and looked somewhat bewildered, so I thought it best to make sure of what quarters I could get and went up to my friends of the 42nd. They had got dinner ready: some soup that you would have emptied into the slop pail, but which was very greedily devoured, cold salt beef and a piece of cold chicken, all diluted with rum and brackish water. We had a good pot of hot tea made, and as the sun set went down to the bottom of the cliff and had a good swim.

There were no tents to sleep in, and so we made a kind of canopy by stretching a plaid over a table-top set on edge, and fastening the four corners to sticks driven into the ground. Our blankets were laid on the ground. After some rum and water and a pipe we turned in. It was very comfortable except that we were overrun with ants, and now and then a bullet came whistling past. I know that my slumbers were very sound. During the night the French set some houses in the town on fire and a fatigue party of English had to go down and put it out, which they did by pulling the houses down on each side of them. After breakfast I went down to the sea again to see the soldiers bathe. They went in by regiments; when the officers with them thought they had been in long enough they were called out by sound of trumpet and another regiment took their place.

Colonel Gordon sent for me to say that they had arranged for me to live in the same room with himself, Colonel Airey and Hallewell, and asked me to take some sketches of the place for Lord Raglan. We four slept in the same room and Colonel Brownrigg in the next.

It is decided that the army stops here ten days to erect works for the defence of the place, which the Turks are to occupy. The small steamers are all gone into the Sea of Azov looking out for information and for prizes, of which several have already been taken. The value of Yenikale to the allies is immense, as they now cut off all supplies coming to the Russians from Asia and down the Sea of Azov, and can from here make attacks upon any port of the Asiatic coast of the Black Sea, or the ports of the Sea of Azov. It is possible they may send an expedition to Anapa, but the uncertainty is so great and my anxiety to get home so strong, that I have this morning applied for a passage back to Balaclava by the first steamer that leaves, and one will have to go soon to carry dispatches.

RETURN TO HEADQUARTERS

Kamiesch Bay, May 30th 1855.

We have just dropped anchor here. I left yesterday in a little steamer that took us down to the "Royal Albert" where I waited till twelve at night while Admiral Lyons [Rear-Admiral Sir (later Lord) Edmund Lyons, second in command of the Fleet] wrote his dispatches to the Government. You will learn from the papers the results of the expedition, so I will say nothing about it. I left Hallewell in high spirits, looking forward to a cruise to Anapa. He had just got three cases of wine and was lifted up accordingly.

Headquarters,
June 2nd 1855.

I wish to tell you that I got back safe last night. I dined with Lord Raglan today. I did not get the invitation till 8 o'clock, the hour named for dinner, as I had been for a long ride to the plain of Baidar and the new country now open to us by the advance of the army to the river Tchernaya. I never beheld anything more beautiful than the plain of Baidar, covered with high vegetation, with dark woods, and closed in all round with rugged mountains. There are two villages in the plain, but both were in ruins, and we could not see a single soul in the whole valley. We returned across the Sardinian camp to the Tchernaya about eight miles from Sebastopol, at a point where it comes out of the hills. We crossed the river at a ford where I, being in advance, popped horse and all into a deep hole. We soon scrambled out and got well laughed at and had to ride home damp.

On our way we went exactly in the line taken by our cavalry at Balaclava [25th October 1854], except that we met instead of following their line of advance. We came upon many skeletons half buried, one was lying as if he had raised himself upon his elbow, the bare skull sticking up with still enough flesh left in the muscles to prevent it falling from the shoulders; another man's feet and hands were out of the ground, the shoes on his feet, and the flesh gone.

When I got to Headquarters I found Lord Raglan's invitation to dinner, changed my things as quickly as possible, and then had to wait with the rest till quarter past ten. When we sat down Lord Raglan placed me on his left hand and made me give accounts of the expedition to Kertch. He spoke very highly of Hallewell and said that Sir George Brown calls him "his eyes" and places the greatest confidence in him.

While at dinner, a dispatch came from Sir E. Lyons stating that the fleet had up to that time taken or destroyed 240 Russian vessels in the Sea of Azov, that they had landed at Ghenitchesk at the end of the long slip of land that runs north from the Crimea to the mainland, and had destroyed six million rations provided for the Russian army, with the loss of only one man. [Flour and corn rations for four months for 100,000 men—including what the Russians had themselves destroyed to prevent it falling into the hands of the allies.]

The bombardment of Sebastopol begins again in a few days, and everyone believes that this time the south side will be taken. This Kertch affair is a terrible blow to them.

Headquarters,
June 4th/55.

I wrote you a short note by the last mail to tell you that I had got back from Yenikale all safe. After posting it I went down to Balaclava and varnished a lot of negatives, and went in a boat to the sea outside the harbour for a bathe. Most glorious it is, taking a leap out of a boat into the clear deep water. Lots of people go towards evening and the sea is quite studded with boats of bathers and anglers. In coming back I passed a steamer with soldiers on board, and seeing 88 marked on some of their caps I asked if Captain Maynard [Fenton's brother-in-law] were on board. "To be sure he is", was the answer, so I climbed up and found him in the cabin sitting over his wine. He did not know me for I am rather fierce-looking just now, my face is as red as a soldier's jacket and my linen shirt has been succeeded by a red flannel one. Edmund is very pleased at getting out.

Yesterday being Sunday [3rd June] I went to morning service at a little wooden church. There was one lady present, Mrs. Estcourt, General Estcourt's wife. It was quite a refreshing sight, her white bonnet and muslin fall among the warlike dresses around. I enjoyed much listening to the church service once more. What a contrast its peaceful spirit is to the harsh scenes of violence and suffering one sees all round!

After service I set off with Angel and Captain Chetwoode for a ride. We went beyond Kamara for a mile or so to a little chapel on the hill, and then turned away to the right till we reached a fountain we had noticed two days before. There we rested and let our horses get their fill of the long rich grass in which they were nearly hidden.

In an hour or so we went down towards the Tchernaya. I tried to cross the ford and had nearly got over when a sentry shouted to me to come back. I did not hear him for the rush of the water, but Angel shouted out my name, and on looking round I saw the man had snatched up his musket and was pointing it at me. I have had many rows with the French sentries; they are brutal to everyone, their own people not excepted. Being in civilian's dress I am much exposed to their rudeness, but as yet, I am happy to say, I have always been able to set them down.

The Sardinians are quite a pleasant contrast in their behaviour to the French. After a very nice bathe we were riding along the bank when we saw a struggle in the water. We hurried up and saw one fellow struggling to the bank and another disappearing under the water. While the Sardinians were calling out for help, several of us were off our horses and getting rid of our clothes, but Donald Campbell, of the next hut to ours, jumped in with all his clothes on and without taking his spectacles off; another officer jumped in horse and all, but Campbell caught the Sardinian by the head and pulled the poor fellow out. He was nearly gone, but we got him round at last. It was rather a droll sight, when we saw that he was recovering. An Englishman who was bathing on the other side had swum over and was bustling about, I had nothing on but boots and shirt, Campbell had stripped and was drying his clothes, the other officer the same, and the Sards vociferating. When the man had quite got round they brought him to thank Campbell, which as neither spoke the other's language was not a very lucid thanksgiving. However, wishing to speak in intelligible language, the man pulled out his purse and wanted Campbell to take it!

Tuesday [5th June]. Yesterday morning I went to breakfast with General Pélissier. The horse I am riding (one of Hallewell's) had broken loose in the night, Sparling having been drunk and not fastened him properly. Three men went out to find him, but I saw no more of him that day and had to borrow a nag and a patched-up saddle with stirrups too short, to go a mile to the headquarters of the French army. We were twenty at breakfast in a darkened hut, General Rose, Captain Foley and two other Englishmen being of the party. It was rather stupid, General Pélissier kept all the conversation to himself, and his conversation is not brilliant. He is a very good personification of the French army, for he is rough in his manners, though not without a certain *bonhomie*. He cares nothing for the sacrifice of life, and does not seem troubled with scruples of any kind. His face has an expression of brutal boldness something like that of a wild boar. However, he is coming to-morrow at 5 a.m. to have his likeness taken: I mean to have a good one of him (*Pl. 68*).

LORD RAGLAN'S DINNER PARTY

I and Angel were invited to dine with Lord Raglan. Lady G. Paget was there; she is very pretty and is at present the *belle* of the Crimea. Lord George Paget was there too, and for once got very chatty; champagne had something to do with it. I was on Lord Raglan's right and Lady George on his left, so I had plenty of conversation with her. Prince Edward of Saxe-Weimar was there too. He is a very nice quiet fellow, plain but a good figure, and seems a great favourite here. In honour of the lady's presence we had rather a swell dinner. While at table a telegraphic message came to say that poor Admiral Boxer was very ill of cholera and not expected to recover. He died at midnight, and no one was ever more regretted, for he was a universal favourite and had done an immense deal for the improvement of Balaclava.

I am afraid of the preparations for coming away; remembering the trouble I had in disembarking I do not like the prospect of going through it all again, and in such hot weather, too. Sparling is gone down today to pack up boxes of negatives. There are very few vessels going straight to England and I must get one that does, to send the men and baggage by, even if I come home myself via Marseilles, which I shall try to do.

To William Agnew.

Headquarters,
Monday, June 4th 1855.

I have just received a message from Mr. Smith, post master at Constantinople, to say that he found great difficulty in getting back the photographs from the Embassy, and that he had at last been obliged to write a very peremptory letter to Mr. Alison, secretary of regulation, in order to recover them. You will doubtless have received them by this time.

I am now at Headquarters taking a few portraits I am yet in want of. Lord Raglan gave me a sitting this morning and I have obtained a very good likeness of him (*Pl. 65*). General Pélissier, with whom I breakfasted this morning, is coming the day after tomorrow at five in the morning. It is impossible to work after nine or ten from the intense heat, which sends the stoppers flying out of my bottles, and spoils every picture. I am almost at the end of my materials, having only 1 oz. of nitrate of silver left, and should be away if it were not for these great guns, each of whose portrait has to be fairly hunted down. I don't think I shall get General Canrobert's likeness as he is away at Tchorgoun with the part of the army recently sent out in that direction. I have got W. H. Russell's likeness (*Pl. 43*). The sanitary commission (*Pl. 41*) have left.

As for your question about the name of the picture, General Barnard says you are quite safe in calling it the "Siege of Sebastopol", as there is little doubt that the south side will soon be taken. Pélissier is thoroughly in earnest, and when any attack does not succeed to his mind, he sends the same troops to do it over again. The expedition to Kertch has been a great blow to the Russians. I was with it, and everyone was astonished at the little defence that was made of so important a point. I took two water-colour sketches of Yenikale.

This morning we have the news that the Russians had abandoned Sujak Kale, leaving us 60 guns and 85 mortars. The complete stoppage of the supplies of the Russian army coming from the Sea of Azov will compel them soon to evacuate the Crimea, even if not soon driven out. If the attack on Anapa succeeds, Sir G. Brown's expedition will have nothing left to desire. Hallewell is Quartermaster-General of the reinforcements which left here three days since for Sir G. Brown's, and I have no doubt that in two days' time we shall hear of the attack on Anapa. It is said that all the Russian forces in Circassia are concentrating there. If true, there will be a tough contact there, though our men are so new that there can be little doubt of the result if once they come to close quarters. [The Russians evacuated Anapa on 5th June, and this important news was brought to Sir George Brown at Kertch by Captain Hughes—*Pl. 66*.]

I shall bring the negatives with me, as it would not be safe to send them, and to get them home uninjured, even with my own supervision, will cause much trouble unless I am lucky enough to get them shipped in a vessel going straight to England. I sent you a packet of portraits some days since; probably before leaving I shall send you another.

To his brother Joseph.

June 9th 1855.

I got your note yesterday and have just time before post to answer it. Agnew distresses himself for nothing. He is sure to make lots of money by the transactions; even I could. As for sending him the negatives, he does not know what he asks.

They would be ruined in a fortnight in the hands of anybody he could get to print them. Besides, they are not all his. I shall start from here as soon as I can sell my things and get a passage.

CAPTURE OF THE MAMELON AND THE QUARRIES

On 7th June the French, commanded by General Bosquet, took the Mamelon, were driven out, and recaptured it. Their total casualties that day were 5,543. It was arranged that as soon as the French had carried the Mamelon, the English, commanded by Colonel Shirley of the 88th, should attack the quarries and the fieldwork covering them, in front of the Redan. The fight for the quarries lasted nearly ten hours and finally the English were left in possession; their casualties amounted to 693 men.

We have had awful fighting here the day before yesterday. The French took the Mamelon and lost, so say the aides-de-camp at Headquarters, 4,000 men. I have written the whole account to Grace [see next letter], she will send copies, but I have understated both their and our own loss in taking the quarries. We lost, it is now said, 600 men. The prisoners we have taken say that they have lost 25,000 men, it appears incredible, 15,000 in the assault, and the other 10,000 in the bombardment of the afternoon and of the morning before the assault took place. I cannot but think they have much exaggerated their loss [Russians lost 5,000 in the fighting, and 3,507 in the preliminary bombardment], but still it must be frightful, for they were all drawn up behind the three points of attack in dense columns to repulse the expected attack, and the fire from our batteries was something such as the world never heard of.

88th Regt., June 8th 1855.

The bombardment of Sebastopol recommenced the day before yesterday [6th June] at three in the afternoon. I had gone to General Bosquet and was on my way there when suddenly all the batteries on our side began to send forth puffs of white smoke, and soon the air was ringing with the increasing din. It was seven minutes before the Russian guns replied. The fire was far more rapid than the last time and the guns heavier and nearer the town, so that before evening it was very plain that many of the enemy's guns were silenced and their works much knocked about. I went to dine with Bosquet and reached his quarters just as he returned from a ride through his troops, who cheered him with great vehemence. He settled after dinner that if the reports from the batteries continue the next morning to be favourable, the French should attack the Mamelon in the evening.

Next morning at Headquarters I heard the Light Division would be called out either to support the French or to attack a different point, so set out, as I felt anxious about Captain Corbett and Edmund [Maynard] who had promised to come and breakfast with me. On my way I went round by the different places where a good view of the firing was to be had. I was much pleased to see the great difference between the result of this and of the last bombardment.

At the 88th I found that all the officers were ordered to stay in camp as they might be wanted. I promised to dine with Corbett; as a lot of fellows called in and he had just received a case of claret, everybody got very merry. There were several collected in his tent discussing what was likely to be done, when an orderly came round with a paper directing that Major Bailey should form a body of 100 men on a storming party and should take with him Captains Maynard (second in command), Beresford and Lieut. Grier, and that Captain Corbett should take 150 men as a reserve with Captain Wray and other officers, and that they should be ready at four o'clock.

At first the news was received in silence, for everybody knew that it promised a terrible encounter, but soon excitement overcame apprehension and everybody set to work in high spirits to prepare. It was nearly four and there was no time to get dinner, so each one snatched up what he could. I made Edmund take something, and did my best to see that all should go out in a fit state of body to encounter fatigue.

Corbett said when we were alone, "Now Roger, my boy, we could not breakfast with you today, but if we come out all right Edmund and I will brush you up tomorrow at six, and you shall take our likenesses." He ordered dinner to be got ready for me; I was too anxious to wait for it, so took part of an omelette that was ready and prepared to march a little way with them. Before setting out he said to me, "Roger, just stand sentry at my door for a bit, while I read a little", and he read in his Bible, I taking care that no one entered. Just then an officer came up with some money for him and he paid off a few debts and said, "Now then, if I don't get back, mind I don't owe anybody a shilling, and that's more than some of you can say, my boys." I dare not go to Edmund for I knew that he would be thinking of his mother, as I was, and I did not wish to agitate him; besides, I knew that he did not need reminding that in the midst of life we are in death.

While they were falling in, I went down to the edge of the ravine down which the troops were to march to the trenches before the attack. The French columns were approaching, Zouaves leading; as they drew near, our soldiers not on duty stood as a hedge on either side and cheered each regiment as they passed. Most of the French seemed wild with excitement, though some looked very anxious, and well they might, for it was certain that many of those voices cheering so loudly would be still in death before the sun had set. When they had passed I went back to our columns, and heard General Pennefather going amongst the men begging them not to shout, as they were only giving the Russians notice of what was coming. At the 88th I found Edmund staying with his company, and beside him, instead of Grier, a fine young fellow named Webb, who had begged of the Colonel to allow him to go with the storming party instead of the reserve. He told me that he wished to go with Edmund. Soon Colonel Shirley came up and shook hands with me, and then gave the order to Major Bailey, who cantered up and called out, "Now Edmund, make your men move on." I went with them a little way down the ravine and when they halted there, shook hands with Edmund, praying silently that the hand of God might protect him in the battle.

There was no place where the English attack on the quarries could be seen, so I went up to the look-out of our three-mortar battery to watch the French assault the Mamelon. For an hour we waited and nothing could be seen. The fire of our batteries was slack, but the Russians fired over our heads and from every gun they could use, and from their ships, in order to hit the troops in their advance, for it was evident that the intention to assault was known.

At last with our glasses we could see the French troops creeping along the inside of their advanced trenches, which seemed to get blacker and blacker as the stream of men wound round the inside. A rocket went up from the Victoria Redoubt on our right, and immediately every gun in our trenches and in the French lines began to vomit out a stream of shot and shell, the smoke from which, condensing down, formed far away to seaward a thick pall which the sun's rays could scarcely penetrate. This fire lasted, as far as I can remember, ten minutes or a quarter of an hour; while it lasted, probably nothing more terrific was ever heard or seen. Then the French began to swarm across their own trenches and rush up the hillside to the Mamelon. There was a sharp musketry fire for a few minutes and then I saw first one or two, then half a dozen, and then scores on the top of the parapet and leaping into the interior. For a time there was a sharp rattle of musketry, and the flashes began to show in the twilight.

Soon we saw them engaging on the other side and rushing up to the Malakoff: well done the French! Then, however, we saw that there was a check: instead of climbing the parapet as at the Mamelon, they spread themselves out in the front and kept firing away without advancing. From the interior, globes of fire, bursting with a thousand sparkles, were constantly hurled amongst them, rifles spat out their fire, and one or two guns still fit for use ploughed their ranks. Their line got thinner, I saw fellows stealing away back to the Mamelon, and in a few minutes the attacking force seemed to have melted away to nothing.

There was a slight pause, but while congratulating each other that at least the Mamelon was taken, musketry was heard on the other side of it and I saw something like a dark serpent coming up the hill leaving the Russian trenches. While we were trying to believe this was a French reinforcement, the stragglers began coming out of the Mamelon, then a crowd and then the whole body were hurrying down the hill. The breastwork of the Mamelon was crowded with Russians firing into their retreating enemy, the heavy guns which had partially stopped began again, and the Malakoff as a sort of bravado fired a gun at us as we looked on.

A mortar at the left of it had been firing at us all the time, for we were a conspicuous group, and their missiles kept coming over our heads, each time clearing us more narrowly. Several round shot, too, whizzed past, and a few went right through amongst us, being sufficiently spent for us to see them and get out of their way. One poor fellow, a navvy, got confused, I suppose, when the cry arose of "Here's a round shot, look out!", and was struck on the side of the head and killed on the spot. A Sardinian officer had his sword torn from his side by another shot, but was not hurt. I never thought I could have been so indifferent while shells were bursting in front, on each side and behind, but the absorbing interest in the struggle before us almost conquered every feeling of fear.

After a pause of half an hour during which we were all exceedingly distressed at the defeat the French had sustained, a trumpet in their trenches sounded the *pas de charge*. Again a swarm of men issued from the lines and advanced to the attack, there was a short but firm fire at the edge of the parapet, and then we thought that we could see one of the figures on the parapet against the blue sky waving a flag and beckoning the assailants on, and soon a few men were seen jumping into the inside. By degrees the parapet was clear but the fire inside seemed gradually to retreat; it was evident the French had retaken the fort.

While this was going on, an A.D.C. came up with a piece of paper to General Codrington [Major-General Sir William John Codrington] who commands the Light Division in General Brown's absence. He read it and instantly mounted and rode off, ordering all officers of the Light Division present to follow him. We soon learned that the English were hard pressed and that Colonel Shirley, who commanded the attack, had written to say he could not hold the quarries which he had taken unless reinforcements were sent to him. I waited a little longer to see if the French were likely to hold their conquest, and finding they seemed secure, thought I would go down to the 88th and see if any news had come up.

CASUALTIES AMONG FENTON'S FRIENDS

I made straight for Edmund's tent and found him there in bed talking to the Dr., his arm bound up and his right hand stained with blood. He had been shot through the arm, but no bone was touched or artery injured. The wound was dressed and he was looking very cheerful though rather pale, faint and thirsty. I made him up at once a drink of lemon juice, water and sugar, with a little of Corbett's claret to revive him. He drank it off greedily, and then I got him some hot tea and he seemed as comfortable as the increasing pain would permit him to be. The Dr. says that his wound is not dangerous and will most likely leave nothing more than a mark upon him.

When we were alone he told me that when they rushed into the pits he was the second man in, an officer of the 77th being before him. At first he was only followed by one sergeant, who said to him, "Captain Maynard, I'll follow you anywhere"; it was not until he shouted to his men that the Russians were retreating, that the men followed in. So many of them are quite boys that it is not surprising. After holding the pits while the Russians returned to the charge, and being flanked, they had to halt. Edmund says that while rallying his men for the second attack he felt himself hit and got confused and faint, and immediately grew very thirsty. He was carried out by two men on a stretcher, but feeling great pain from the motion he got up and walked the greater part of the way, getting a glass of water when he got to the first tents. He could not tell me anything about the rest.

The Dr. told me that Major Bailey in the next hut was hit through the stomach and it was evident that he considered him in great danger. Officers kept coming up to see Edmund and to bring scraps of news. Meanwhile I got a blanket out of Corbett's hut, laid it on the ground, and borrowing another, made up a bed in Edmund's tent. When we were alone he asked me to read to him something out of the Bible, so I read the 103rd and other similar Psalms. I am sure we were both heartily grateful to God for his mercy in sparing Edmund's mother the sorrow of losing her dear son. Bye and bye an officer came in to say that Webb was killed, poor fellow. When he told me he had got leave to go with Edmund I looked at his handsome face and felt horrified at the idea of his thus offering himself up for slaughter. His body has not been found but it is said to be lying on the hillside close to the parapet of the Redan.

Meanwhile wounded men were going past, some carried, others staggering along to their own quarters, groaning and asking for water, or faintly asking their way. Towards eleven a detachment of a hundred men who had been sent down to act as support if needed, came back and brought the news that poor Corbett had been shot through the head and killed on the spot while leading up the reserve, and that Wray also was missing when the muster roll was called. As no certainty could be obtained I determined to get Edmund quiet for the night; the Dr. gave him an opiate and I mixed up for him a large cup of cooling drink and shut up the tent. He did not sleep, however, though I could not help doing so. Early this morning I got him some cocoa and a biscuit and then set off to Headquarters to let them know where I was. On my return I found poor Corbett's body in his tent, lying on the bed where twenty-four hours before he had been lolling in the full enjoyment of life, with a hearty relish for fun. Wray was also lying dead in the next tent, a cheerful winning-looking fellow who seemed made for life and happiness. Out of five officers of the 88th who were in Corbett's tent when the order came to fall in, three were killed, one wounded, and only one unhurt. That one, Beresford, came up at that moment from the trenches covered with dust, his clothes torn, his boots split across, and haggard-looking eyes. He told us how the Russians had met them when they advanced, in front and on both flanks, and how Corbett on one side and Wray on the other had fallen dead almost together. You will not be surprised that I feel wretched about their loss, having been so intimate with them. In an hour I am going to see them laid in their last resting place.

It is said that the French will attack the Malakoff tower and our men the Redan. The tower is on fire in several places. The French have had hard work all day connecting the Mamelon with their own lines, and our men, I suppose, have been doing the same in the quarries. The batteries have been throwing shell into the Redan and Malakoff, which have kept quiet, most likely reserving their efforts for tonight.

Poor Bailey died at midnight after great suffering. The 88th lost four officers killed and three wounded. It is said there are forty officers in the Light Division killed and wounded: how many men we do not yet know. Edmund will perhaps have to go home, certainly he will if he wishes, and before he can get fit for duty the hard fighting before Sebastopol will be over.

I have done my work and have nothing to do but look out for a vessel. I am much hindered by Sparling, who has been drinking a great deal lately and has in consequence a bad attack of dysentery which has laid him on the shelf.

June 9th. Just after I left off writing, Lord Raglan came up and enquired for the wounded officers. He came to Edmund's tent and shook hands with him, asking him how he was. He stayed about five minutes and then shook hands and went away. Colonel Shirley came up from the trenches about the same time; he says the attack was most splendid and well managed throughout. I gather from all I heard that it was after taking the rifle pits [quarries] and a work in advance of them that they were short of ammunition. As the Russians advanced in great numbers, Major Bailey withdrew the men to the rifle pits which they had taken. The Russians still advanced, however, and Bailey and Edmund called out, "Come on, 88th", and charged them with the bayonet and drove them back. Then Bailey and Edmund again withdrew their men to the rifle pits to wait for ammunition. Edmund saw a place where a few men could annoy the Russians much, and went to ask the Colonel to let him put some men there. He had placed some and was going back to bring some more when he was struck.

THE UNSUCCESSFUL ATTACKS ON THE MALAKOFF AND REDAN

The French and English having on 7th June occupied the Mamelon and the quarries respectively, the final stage was to take the Malakoff and the Redan, which had been protected by the Mamelon and quarries. The fourth bombardment started on Sunday 17th June. General Pélissier informed Lord Raglan that he needed two hours after dawn to continue the bombardment in order to destroy what the Russians would have repaired during the night, before sending in attacking troops at five or 5.30. Pélissier, however, abruptly reversed his plans without consulting Raglan (though he did, of course, inform him) and omitted the preliminary bombardment. This was a terrible error of judgment, due to over-confidence in the destruction that had been wrought on the Russians. It was followed by another unfortunate mistake. General Mayran thought that a shell with a trail of light from its fuse was the rocket signalling the attack, and led on his forces prematurely thus dislocating all the arrangements for simultaneous action. The French swarmed up the Malakoff but were driven back, and Lord Raglan felt obliged to support the French by starting the English attack on the Redan at once without having made a preliminary bombardment. The British had to advance over 470 yards of open ground. In two unsuccessful assaults on the Redan they lost 717 men and 64 officers, including the two commanders who led the attacks, General Sir John Campbell and Colonel Yea. The total British losses that day in killed, wounded and missing amounted to 1,505, French casualties 3,500, Russian 1,500 (they had lost 4,000 in the previous day's bombardment).

June 18th 1855.

We have just passed through what seems to be a hideous dream. Last night after a continuous and apparently successful bombardment of twenty-four hours it was resolved that the assault on the Malakoff should be made by the French and on the Redan by the English, early in the morning. Everyone seemed to be certain of success. "Stop over tomorrow", I heard everyone say, "and you will see at last the inside of Sebastopol." We had a merry evening, everyone anticipating a short though perhaps sharp struggle and a triumphant close to this terrible siege. Those who ventured to hint that the place was strong, its defenders brave men and that they might give us some trouble yet, were few and unheard.

The attack was to be made with the first blush of dawn. Few of us went to bed. I slept for a couple of hours but rose at half past one, got a cup of tea, and with two others set off on horseback in the dark across to Cathcart's Hill, where an excellent view of the attack on the Redan was to be obtained. Lord Raglan was out at two and went down into the advanced trenches. When we got to the ground, twilight was just appearing. We went down the hill towards the batteries and found a few more spectators sitting on the grass looking through the mist to make out the outlines of the town. As the light began to dawn, the dark mass of the Redan began to show dimly above the fog. The batteries were firing hard, the town was on fire in three places, a lurid smoke rose curling above the white cloud that enveloped all the batteries. The Mamelon could scarcely be seen, but its place was indicated by the flashes rising from it, and the Malakoff was quite invisible, but shells continually breaking over it showed us where it was.

Before sunrise a rocket rose perpendicularly from Fort Victoria and instantly there began a rattle of musketry which rolled round the base of the Malakoff, now seeming to climb its side and again receding, but growing louder every minute. We could see nothing, not even the outline of the hills, and could only judge of the progress of the conflict by the sound of the musketry. Meanwhile our batteries kept up a very sharp fire of shell and every two minutes a rocket rushed up behind us with a roar and glided through the sky into the town. The sun rose and began to dissipate the mist, and the Mamelon came out pretty clear, and by degrees the Malakoff's battered summit, furrowed with the craters where shell had burst, but spitting out fire from every aperture. The French were hidden by one of our batteries intervening, and every eye was strained to catch a glimpse of them swarming up the steep sides of the Malakoff. When they did succeed in getting high enough up for us to see them we could see Russian officers standing on the parapet braving the fire and pointing to their men where to aim their guns.

After a while, in front of us rose another rattle of musketry, indicating that our troops were attacking the Redan. It was difficult to distinguish how matters were going on, for the musketry was incessant and as it became faint on one side it became louder on another, but still we could see flashes from both the forts, showing that the Russians were still in possession. The first onset of the French evidently failed, for their fire diminished, then it renewed again and through the smoke a flag was unfurled on the top of the Malakoff and we all cried out, "They're in at last; now for the Redan!", but we were soon undeceived: the flag was hoisted by the Russians, either as a defiance, or more probably to let their batteries know that they were still in possession and to prevent them from firing into it. The attack seemed to be several times renewed, but each time the musketry was fainter.

By this time it was eight o'clock. The wind had risen and cleared away the mist and in the clear morning sun we could see everything that stirred. I could see with my glass our storming party clustering like bees in the quarries and lying in long black lines under the shelter of the trenches taken from the Russians last week. Nearer, behind our batteries, lay a double line of redcoats ready to go in as a reserve, and when it was evident that both we and the French had been beaten back, the Guards and Highlanders were marched in to act as a reserve for a final attack.

While waiting to see the result of this, sad rumours began to spread among the crowd of officers and spectators gathered in large crowds along the edge of Cathcart's Hill. Sir J. Campbell, my kind host of six weeks ago, was said to be killed. Soon the rumours became a certainty, and gloom was seen on every face, for no man was more beloved by the whole army than Sir John. Bye and bye slightly wounded men came up supported by the other soldiers, and the tale they told confirmed all our fears. Our men had attacked twice and been driven back each time by a frightful fire of grape. Next an officer was borne up on a litter. They had spread green boughs over his face to keep the sun from him. His foot was broken. Soon the wounded men came up in numbers.

After waiting an hour and there being no signs of an immediate renewal of the attack, I accepted an invite to breakfast from Lieut. Gough of the Naval Brigade. On the way to his hut an ambulance came up and in it a naval officer named Cave, shot through the thigh. He said to Gough it had been a disgraceful attack, no management, no orders. We saw him to his tent and sat down to breakfast. Litter after litter came pouring in, bringing wounded men to the hospital. One poor fellow, a seaman, was brought in dead. Gough spoke of him as one of his best men, so I went to look at him. One could scarcely believe he was dead, he seemed just to be resting a little. Beside him lay sewn up in a blanket a sailor killed yesterday in my sight by a fragment of shell. I went into the hospital. It was an awful sight, but I will not shock you with the description.

Returning to breakfast—and it is an odd thing that in the midst of all these horrors no one loses his appetite—news kept dropping in, first of one officer then of another of the Naval Brigade being wounded. We had scarcely heard of the escape of one named Kidd when he was brought in mortally wounded by a shot through the chest. He had got through the fight and was quite happy and elated at his escape, when he saw some of our men lying outside the trench, and in the attempt to drag them in got his death wound. We went into the hospital where he lay, poor fellow. He turned his glazing eyes upon us and then closed them, panting heavily for breath. He died in a few minutes. Out of sixty of the Naval Brigade only twelve came out unhurt. News kept coming up of well-known names that were henceforth to be only memories. Colonel Yea was killed by the same shot that took off poor Sir John Campbell's head. Colonel Tylden was shot through both thighs, and several regiments suffered terribly in their officers.

Going back to Cathcart's Hill there came up a terrible storm of wind, sweeping up a cloud of dust that darkened the whole air. The crowd of spectators had disappeared, and we heard that there was to be no further attack. I went on to see Hallewell, found him lying in his tent trying to keep up his spirits with a bottle of champagne. He was taken with bad spasms in a few minutes and we had to rub his limbs hard for some time before he came round. It was the effect of hard work and no sleep, he is not hurt. I then went to Edmund. He is up and getting on nicely and would soon be well but that his wound runs very much and keeps him weak.

Such is our anniversary of the 18th of June. In our confidence of success we had chosen this day, it is said, that on the anniversary of Waterloo a victory common to both nations might efface from the minds of one the recollection of their former defeat, but we reckoned too proudly, and now the 18th of June will be a glorious day to the Russians.

19th. I have just got news of the "Rinoco" being about to return and am going to try to get home by her. There is no talk of a fresh assault. It is said now that both French and English will have to work their way by sap into the two forts. The 38th and one other regiment, it seems, carried the part of the enemy's position for which they were appointed, but the rest having been ruined, they could not move forward, and would have been annihilated had they tried to return in daylight. They got back to our trenches last night at ten, having sheltered themselves during the day as well as they could among the ruined houses that cover the slope on the left of the Redan.

Our loss is not yet known, but the 18th, 38th, 57th and 44th have suffered very severely. It is supposed that we have lost near 1,500 men and the French 5,000. They always attack in much greater numbers than we do and so suffer more. Our engineers say that the defeat was owing to General Pélissier's advancing the attack by two hours, thus preventing our batteries from silencing the guns which the Russians had got into the Redan during the night, so that our men when they advanced from the trenches were met with a tremendous fire of grape. I incline to think that the failure of the attack was not owing to General Pélissier but to our own presumption in undervaluing the resistance to be expected.

What's to be done now no one can guess, except that it will now be a long time before the town is taken. Engineer officers say that we must go at it again; other officers say that we shall never take it till the last engineer officer is hanged, and that the proper way is to lick the enemy at Simferopol [to the north-east of Sebastopol] and then invest the town. Captain Peel, who was wounded yesterday close to the ditch of the Redan, says that it cannot be taken. The men generally do not seem discouraged, but their loss has been small in comparison with that of the officers. Last night a soldier of the 89th came up and asked to see Lord Raglan. Colonel Steele asked what he wanted, and was told that the privates of the regiment had asked him to offer on their part to storm the Redan if he would give them a regiment as support.

It is awfully hot again now, one drinks like a fish. I reckoned yesterday that I took seventeen tumblers of liquid, nine of which were tea, two champagne and the rest beer. If this army is distinguished by any character from all others we read of in history, it is that it is a perspiring one. Our clothes are always wringing wet and we are obliged to wash all over twice a day. Well, I shall be able, I hope, in a very short time to tell you all these things instead of writing them, so good bye.

THE RETURN TO ENGLAND

Istania, Bosphorus.
June 25th.

I told you in my last letter that I should probably start by the "Rinoco". Well, I received a message that the ship was to go next day, being that appointed for the sale of my things. I expected it would go suddenly, for those vessels are often ordered off at an hour's notice, so I made Sparling and William pack hard the night before, as they thought, very uselessly. I sold most of the heavy things, but one horse would not go off, and my best too. There was only £10 offered for him, and lots of other horses were sent up for sale, none of which were sold. There have been so many officers killed that there is a perfect glut of such things as are wanted in camp. I put my van up but only £26 was offered for it. I withdrew it very reluctantly, as I did not know how to get it on board. After the sale was over, the agent of Mr. D. came and offered £30 for it, but I refused as I should have to make another when I returned; finally I sold it for £35. I then sent the horse to Hallewell to be sold when a chance occurred, and then I went to bid good bye to Edmund. I left him a tin containing several pounds of those beautiful biscuits, six pounds of coffee and about half a dozen bottles of wine, with several other things. He is quite hearty and in high spirits.

Getting back to Headquarters by three, I received a message by telegraph that the vessel would leave Balaclava by four o'clock. Trusting that four would be eight, I packed my clothes, paid my bills, and loaded the van, and set off on my road to Primrose Hill in high glee, cracking jokes with everybody I met, for I have as many acquaintances here as the parish pump. Just outside Balaclava I met Stopford, who was going by the same ship. He pulled a long face and called out I was just five minutes too late, the "Rinoco" was off. Well, we went on in a more sober mood to my hut, unloaded the van, gave it our blessing as it went on its way to its new owner, and began to think what was now to be done. Having recommenced the work and packed so as to be ready for any chance, I went out to arrange about getting food for Sparling, William and myself, as we were at present on the wide world. I had invitations from all sides, but I did not know what to do with them. I met Colonel Harding, the Governor [Commandant at Balaclava] and he asked me to dine; I declined. A little further I met Mr. Filder [the Commissary-General]. He has been very ill so I stopped to ask how he was getting on, and in doing so mentioned my disappointment about a vessel. He said, "I have a vessel going to Constantinople tomorrow. I will give you a passage, and there you will most likely find the 'Rinoco'". I eagerly accepted the offer, ran back to the tent, set the men vigorously to work and got them some soup made; next went to tell Colonel Harding that I was going to accept a dinner from him and a bed as well. It was then about seven o'clock, and I found him and his party lounging on his verandah waiting for dinner. We had to wait till nine and I got faint, but we had a jolly meal and then went out to smoke and take coffee outside, all of us in turn falling asleep.

Next morning [22nd June] at half past three I was up, and could get no water to wash, nor a bit of bread to eat as is my usual custom here before going out early. I felt unwell, being attacked with diarrhoea. I got the boxes all put into a boat, and with great exertion of the men—for I felt too ill to do more than look on—got all on board. We had nearly got outside the harbour when I began to vomit, and felt it was not from seasickness. By nine o'clock I was bad with the cholera, and there was no doctor on board. Everybody advised me to take different medicine. I tried rhubarb and peppermint but could not keep it in my stomach, so I got them to make me some rice water and mixed lime juice with it, and while it was preparing drank as much lime juice and water as ever I could, vomiting it all up again every ten minutes, but drinking again so as to keep up the supply of fluid to the blood. At half past ten cramp began in my legs and I had to be held upright and rubbed; in a short time it began in my arms and fingers, which began to turn blue.

I could hardly breathe and felt my eyes staring very much. I never felt much alarmed, but thought as it was possible I might be mistaken about my method of cure, I had better give Sparling and William such directions as might be necessary, especially as I could see that everybody present had a much worse opinion of my chances than I had myself. At noon I felt the tide was turned, for my fingers recovered their colour and the cramp became less violent. I had kept on drinking rice water, and by night the diarrhoea was stopped, though the cramp continued until the middle of the next day. William and Sparling took it in turn to watch me, and I must say they both took great care of me, as well as an old gentleman of the name of Irish who had suggested arrowroot.

I got out of bed the second day to see the entrance to the Bosphorus and got laid on deck, for I felt I could not bear to stand. We lay to that night, and next morning I was up at five to see the Bosphorus. I was somewhat stronger, but still very queer. I enjoyed the sight, but when halfway down, we met the "Rinoco" coming back. We puzzled ourselves with this till the vessel cast anchor; I sent Sparling on shore to enquire. It was Sunday [24th June] and most of the offices were closed, but he learned that she had gone up the Bosphorus to Istania to coal and would be back the next day to proceed on her route. I thought it better to lose no time, so sent Sparling with the Commissary's interpreter to hire a barge to take us and our boxes up the stream; when he did not return I got uneasy when a message came from shore to tell our Captain to get ready to go to sea by four p.m. I set off in a caique with the interpreter to look for Sparling, and found him waiting for the advent of some Turkish boatmen who were with their Padrone at prayers. He then got several caiques, brought them to the vessel, and feeling quite ill, I left Sparling and William to see about the loading.

As soon as the first boat had three or four boxes in the boatmen pushed off and would not come back; William came running to tell me, but it was too late. The next boat I made Sparling get into first, the third boat set off before I could put William into it, the fourth boat had only one rower, and William and I with the rest of our luggage had to get into it and lie down in the bottom for fear of upsetting it. I could not see any of the other boats and felt very anxious, feeling that I was too ill to exert myself as much as was even necessary. We had to pull against the stream, which is very strong. The old boatman, in about an hour, gave in and ran his boat ashore, wanted to be paid for the whole journey and then to divide the load into two boats for the rest of the way. I refused the first proposition, agreed to the second, but when this was settled he and the new boatman began disputing about their share in the prospective pay. This lasted about half an hour, I standing in the sun and getting worse. At last another man rushed up, transferred everything to his boat, and after three hours' work brought us to the "Rinoco". Here I am resting. We leave in a couple of days, and in less than three weeks you may expect to see this skeleton. Meanwhile God bless you. Thine Roger Fenton.

No further attack on the Malakoff and Redan forts guarding the entrance to Sebastopol from the allied positions took place until 8th September, when the French took the Malakoff whilst the English assault on the Redan failed. Considering their position untenable, the Russians retired during the night to the north forts, and the allies entered the city. Although Fenton had not stayed to see the fall of Sebastopol, his brother-in-law Edmund Maynard completes the story with a letter to his mother.

Camp before Sebastopol,
10th Sept. 1855.

Long before this reaches you, you will have heard of our success and of the fall of Sebastopol, that is, of the whole of the south side. The place at present is in flames and has been since Saturday night. The fleet is destroyed and some ships burnt and others sunk, and thousands of Russians in full retreat, marching upon Simferopol it is supposed. Our poor Brigade (the 2nd of the Light Division) has suffered fearfully. We have lost in the 88th one officer killed and ten wounded, and about 150 men killed and wounded out of 396. It has pleased God Almighty to preserve me and it was He alone who shielded me in the hour of danger.

The attack was made on the 8th, commencing at noon. The second Brigade of the Light Division and the second of the second Division were the two selected for the work, and soon after seven in the morning we were marched down to the trenches. The French commenced by attacking the Malakoff, which they took in style, taking the enemy by surprise and entering it without much opposition. The Russians had concentrated the greater part of their force in and near the Redan, fully expecting that that would be the only place of attack, but the French were not left long before an obstinate resistance was opposed to them. Attack after attack was made upon them till nightfall. Still they held their ground manfully without being dislodged in spite of their numerous losses.

As soon as they made an entrance into the place, our storming party, consisting of the 90th and 97th regiments of our Brigade, and the 62nd and 23rd of the second Division, got orders to move on against the Redan, followed by the 19th, 88th, and the 30th and 31st in support of the latter. The scaling ladders were soon fixed and the parapet of the fort mounted by the advanced regiments, when we were brought up at the double, having an open space of 5 or 600 yards from our trenches to the ditch of the Redan to run across; but before we could accomplish this, many of our fellows were swept down by the raking fire which was poured in amongst us. Those of the 88th who were remaining went straight at the ditch, but here were unavoidably mixed up with other regiments when we came to mount the different ladders.

As for myself, the first I came at I went at waving my sword and shouting, I believe, like a madman to urge my company to follow, which they did, but some of the poor fellows were knocked over before they reached the parapet. Many were obstructed by the crowds of men on the bank side. I was scarcely mounted on the top of the parapet myself, before my face was covered with blood and brains spurting from a poor fellow of another regiment who was shot close to me. Such a sight as I must have been for the $2\frac{1}{2}$ hours we remained up there, men falling in every direction and at times almost knocking one over as they fell; then the moans of the poor fellows as they lay at one's feet dying and crying for assistance, but no aid could be given. One object was in view: if possible, to drive the Russians away from behind their parapet, and in endeavouring to accomplish this, dead and dying were alike forgotten and trampled under foot.

Still the enemy could not be driven in. They assailed us with all sorts of missiles and showered us with big stones, bayonets, and every now and then their muskets would come flying in amongst us. We could not bring our men to face it and make a charge over the parapet and jump in amongst the enemy. At one time I endeavoured to get volunteers, determined to lead the way in myself if they would only follow, but this proved a failure; no more than six or eight would enlist for the work. If only fifty or sixty men could have been mustered to follow, it might have been of service and the means of bringing the whole of them in, but to have got in with so few as six or eight would have been sacrificing ourselves to no effect. Officers did their utmost to get the men in, but without effect. At last, in spite of every endeavour, the men became panic struck and made a rush to retire, and it was most fearful to see the way in which they upset and tumbled upon each other in the ditch. I kept my hold on the ladder as long as I could, cheering and trying to keep them up, till at last I was sent head foremost, my left foot catching in one of the bars. For some time I could not extricate myself and was in dread of my left leg being broken; how I managed to get a footing again, I can't say. Afterwards I found that the whole of the heel part of my boot had been torn away and my body covered with bruises, from which I am at present very sore. My old wound also came in for its share of blows, which made it puff up. But a few days, I hope, will see me all to rights again. I received a slight flesh wound on the back of my left hand and should have been returned slightly wounded, but I thought it better not as it would only alarm you unnecessarily seeing it in the newspapers so long before you could hear from me.

After all, it seemed a providential thing that I did not effect an entrance into the Redan, as we have since learnt that the Russians intended to have blown us all up if we had. That same night after they had evacuated it themselves they blew it mostly to pieces.

The Russians destroyed the Redan (Plate 84) and rendered it useless but did not actually blow it up, and on entering it was found that the wounds of the English prisoners had been dressed by the Russians before they evacuated the fort.

We got back to camp at night, the Highland Brigade relieving us in the trenches, and glad I was and thankful to get a stretch and my face washed. My left eye was completely bunged up and my eyebrow singed; I think some sparks must have done it. My jacket was also burnt in many places. It would have puzzled you, dear Mother, to have recognized me coming in in such a state.

I fear I have written you an unintelligible letter, but the late time of the night, and after being hard employed most of the day, must plead my excuse.